VGM Opportunities Series

OPPORTUNITIES IN
BEAUTY CULTURE
CAREERS

Susan Wood Gearhart

Foreword by
Peggi Holmes
President, Cosmetology Teachers of Long Island

VGM Career Horizons
NTC/Contemporary Publishing Company

Cover Photo Credits:
Upper left courtesy of the Museum of Cosmetology; upper right and lower right courtesy of the National Cosmetology Association; lower left courtesy of Pivot Point International, Inc.

Library of Congress Cataloging-in-Publication Data
Gearhart, Susan Wood.
    Opportunities in beauty culture careers / Susan Wood Gearhart.
        p.   cm.—(VGM opportunities series)
    Includes bibliographical references.
    ISBN 0-8442-4610-7 (hard).—ISBN 0-8442-4611-5 (pbk.)
    1. Beauty culture—Vocational guidance.   I. Title.   II. Series.
TT958.G363   1996
646.7'26'02373—dc20   96-1243
                                                                                            CIP

Published by VGM Career Horizons, a division of NTC Publishing Group
4255 West Touhy Avenue
Lincolnwood (Chicago), Illinois 60646-1975, U.S.A.
©1996 by NTC Publishing Group. All rights reserved.
No part of this book may be reproduced, stored in a retrieval
system, or transmitted in any form or by any means,
electronic, mechanical, photocopying, recording or otherwise,
without the prior permission of NTC Publishing Group.
Manufactured in the United States of America.

9 0 VP 9 8 7 6 5 4 3

CONTENTS

About the Author vii

Acknowledgments ix

Foreword xi

Preface xiii

Introduction xv

Dedication xix

1. The Beauty Industry Now 1

Haircutters. Hair colorists. A show of hands. Makeup enhancers. Electrolysis. Research. Management. Cosmetology instructors. Using cosmetology education for other careers. Entrepreneurial cosmetologists. Mobile units.

2. Finding the Right School and Getting Your License 11

School categories. Apprenticeships. Licensing requirements.

3. Cosmetology Curriculum 20

Sample curricula. Specialized courses. Limited certificates. Supplemental courses. Training for instructors. Managerial and business positions.

4. Nail Technicians 34

Licensing and training. Manicuring. Pedicuring. Salaries and working conditions.

5. Positions for Cosmetologists 38

Choosing a place to work.

6. **Beauty Salon Employment** **44**

    Positions in beauty salons.

7. **Aestheticians and Facialists** **50**

    The need for facial specialists. Education for facial specialists. Finding a school and a job. Opening a facial salon. Teaching facial specialty skills.

8. **Makeup artists** **56**

    Skin care. Color. Education. Licensing. Jobs in makeup.

9. **Electrologists** **63**

    Education. Licensing. Finding a job.

10. **Wigs, Hairpieces, and Hair Enhancement** **67**

    Choosing a wig. Working as a wig stylist. Salaries. Selling hairpieces to men.

11. **Beauty Salon Ownership** **71**

    State regulation. Other regulations. Finding a location. Hiring a staff and getting started. The key to success.

12. **Beauty School Ownership** **81**

    Schools of cosmetology regulations. Regulations in California.

13. **Salon Managers and Manager-operators** **93**

    A manager's responsibilities.

14. **Competition Hairstylists** **97**

    Competitions. Reasons for competing.

15. **The Platform Hairstylist** **101**

    The role of the platform stylist. Becoming a platform stylist. Finding a job.

16. **Future Job Outlook for Cosmetologists** **105**

    Job opportunities. Salaries. Working conditions.

17. **State Boards of Cosmetology** **109**

18. **Cosmetology in Canada**...........................113

Hairstyling school. Aestheticians, electrologists, and tattoo artists.
Manicurists and pedicurists. Scalp treatment specialists.
Hairdressing teacher. Finding the right school. Canadian
cosmetological associations.

Appendix A: Bibliography..............................120

Statutes and legal texts. Suggested reading.

Appendix B: Standards for Accreditation 123

Appendix C: Curricula Available in Accredited Schools 125

Appendix D: State Boards of Cosmetology..................131

**Appendix E: Cosmetological Associations
  and Information Sources**...........................139

ABOUT THE AUTHOR

Susan Wood Gearhart is a professional model, dancer, teacher, freelance writer, and editor. She graduated from City University of New York and attended Hiram College, Julliard School, and the Preibar Academy in Berlin. She has modeled for several years for clothing, makeup, and hairstyles. She has developed programs for individual client skin care, skin sensitivity testing, and color coordination.

She has modeled for the major cosmetic firms of Estée Lauder, Clinique, Revlon, Charlie, Shiseido, and Ultima II, and has been a beauty and makeup design consultant for Clinique and Shiseido.

Ms. Gearhart lives in New York City.

ACKNOWLEDGMENTS

My gratitude and appreciation are extended to the following people for their kindness, help, and time. Among those to whom I want to express special thanks are: Daniel Kelley, Ms. Secas, and Cecilia Franco of Christine Valmy, New York City; Leo Galletta and Terry Mazzelli of the Atlas School of Barbering, New York City; Kathleen Paar of Clairol, New York City; Audrey Koppel of Kree Institute of Electrolysis, New York City; Ms. A. Ronni Kolotkin, Certified Electrologist; Mrs. Edith Imre and Mr. Michael of House of Imre, New York City; Ms. Lurlie Calvacca, competition hairstylist and judge for competitions; Carlos Noceda, New York City; Nancy Tynan, Cosmair, Inc., L'Oréal International Salon Institute, New York City; Florence Lacoff, Cosmetological Publishing House, New York City; Margie Estaville, Sacramento, California; Alana Baard and Peggi Holmes, educators; Sheelagh A. McNeill, New York City; and Barbara W. Donner, former editor, NTC Publishing Group, Lincolnwood, Illinois.

FOREWORD

This study in beauty culture opportunities serves two major sectors of the reading population: Teachers, guidance counselors, and their allied professionals; and the future cosmetologists of America.

The numerous references and presentations of information will serve both groups well. It represents a cohesive clearinghouse of information that has previously been scattered in diverse sources. In addition, this data, rather than being presented in a "dry" encyclopedia form, is brought to life literally and figuratively so that it serves as both a reference work and an educational tool.

A career in cosmetology is one of great creativity and glamour. In addition to the skills needed to be successful, you must like being in constant contact with people. Hard work and determination can and will bring you success.

Most of us are unaware as to what it entails to become a cosmetologist.

Each state has different but similar requirements ranging from 1,000 hours to 2,500 hours of education. All states regulate cosmetology schools through State Boards. The State Board establishes the number of hours as well as course curriculum. When the student has satisfied the course requirements, there is a written and practical exam that must be passed to be able to practice. Once you have your cosmetology license, you can pace your career walk according to your needs and speed.

There are many fields of specialties. They include: nail care operator, aesthetician, makeup artist, hair stylist, colorist, chemical permanent wave and straightening specialist, salon managers, and teachers.

You can be anything from a one-person-shop owner in your home to caring for the beauty and cosmetic needs of the stars of stage and screen. Again the choice is yours. How ambitious are you? How committed are you? How dedicated are you? How disciplined are you?

Cosmetology can be a very rewarding and lucrative field. The satisfaction received is enormous, knowing you have changed a person's appearance and helped him or her feel better as well as look better. Remember, if you look good, you feel good, and if you feel good, you will look good.

---◆---

To cosmetologists everywhere

Skill and *Talent* get

Clients into your chair

But, it's your *Attitude* and *Personality*

That keep them there!!

---◆---

I once heard a wise person say, "Find a job you love and you'll never have to work a day in your life."

Peggi Holmes
B.A., Education, City College of New York
M.A., Administration/Education, Hofstra University
Cosmetology Teacher
President of Cosmetology Teachers of Long Island
Member N.C.A.

INTRODUCTION

Employment opportunities in the field of cosmetology have so dramatically changed in the last few years that the increase in need for operators has increased tenfold! It used to be that the numbers of employed cosmetologists remained steady as the individuals moved in and out of the field. Now there is such a demand for hairstylists, manicurists, and cosmeticians that there is an estimated opening of 10,000 new positions to be filled annually. Of course, this includes part-time as well as full-time operators.

The beauty industry has expanded from the small salons and barber shops to full-service boutiques where a client can have a complete head-to-toe makeover. These are sometimes referred to as day spas. The excellent skills of a bevy of operators are put to work to do your hair, legs, fingernails, and toenails simultaneously! As more and more women attain professional positions with impressive commensurate salaries, the demand for beauticians has also burgeoned. The need for top operators to fit into these women's busy schedules has also reshaped the cosmetology industry. House calls have become one innovative way to meet the clients' needs and to raise the prices for your work.

Most cosmetologists work within the confines of a beauty salon which could be anywhere from a tiny one-room shop to a gigantic beauty parlor with dozens of operators. A third of the licensed beauticians own their own salons, while three-quarters of licensed barbers own their own shops. Owning your place of business can obviously increase your earnings tremendously.

There has never been a time when the field of beauty culture has been so exciting. With all the individual needs of varied clientele, you are much more free to seek out your own special niche. Many a hairstylist who started as a novice in the industry is today a high-paid individual with a loyal weekly following.

The variety of specialized beauty services, the advancement of techniques, and the development of numerous hair, skin, and nail products have all had their impact upon the expansion of this labor market. There is simply a greater variety of cosmetologist posts as each area becomes highly specialized. Two areas that have experienced radical development are the hairstylist's and the manicurist's. Both have become so much in demand as creators of fashion and chic that there is often a problem trying to fit all the clients in!

Salaries for working cosmetologists vary radically in this industry because wages are based on location of the salon, level of experience, following, and, of course, how the cosmetologist is actually paid. If salary is based totally on percentage, commission, partial salary, and/or combinations of these financial arrangements, the salary will rise as the salon charges higher rates for its services. Not only does the economy set the standard for these increases, but the demand for fine work has a general effect on the prices that a place of work can charge. The more highly skilled technician has a tremendous advantage over the operator who has merely graduated from cosmetology school and has never kept up with continuing education in the field. Those who choose to apprentice after completing their state boards often find that they eventually earn a salary many times larger than their salaries would have been without the advanced training. Most people are more sophisticated now in their demands for a particular finished hairstyle or makeup, and this puts the burden of knowing how to accomplish that effect on the cosmetologist or cosmetician.

Cosmetology is a field that is as wide open to women as it is to men. The opportunities and potential for advancement are fairly distributed so that your ability and capability will dictate your success. This is a field where you must be self-motivated. There is no one who will push you, so if you desire to have a part-time job for only a few hours of the week, you probably will be able to maintain that arrangement indefinitely. However, if your desire is to build a real career and to meet high goals, this is a perfect field for you to enter, as it offers you a limitless opportunity in your potential for growth.

Both men and women who choose to make cosmetology their chosen career will find it extremely rewarding. It does not have to be a full-time, six-day-a-week, all-out, all-consuming career. You can have a satisfying career in beauty culture even if you work only a few hours a week out of your own home. Nevertheless, the beauty field is an area where you can have a secure future with some of the best salaries in our country today being paid to women. The industry of cosmetology and its myriad jobs are extremely well paid. The jobs are many and challenging, and there is room to move around within certain spheres.

The current shift in employment is toward those with an indispensable technical skill and away from the college graduates. There are new beauty salons opening with regularity, and many positions are available in each one. The statistics show that more cosmetologists are self-employed (own their own salon) than other service workers. The overall outlook for cosmetology as a career is certainly an optimistic one. It is, however, a career where self-motivation is essential. But even for those people who are not interested in owning their own salons, cosmetology offers many opportunities. If you wish to work as a manicurist or hairdresser without the pressure to move upward, cosmetology can still be rewarding. The job is a pleasant one, and the relationship with the patrons can be very satisfying. Any service position is enjoyable if you genuinely like to please people and care about them.

DEDICATION

To Marguerite S. and Wm. Barker Wood,
Gabrielle, Jennifer, and Ted

said that no one likes his or her own hair and that it's just one of those things that you are stuck with. Well, the direct or indirect role of the hairdresser is to help you define your hair more to your liking. This could entail dozens of different procedures, but the most dramatic one is most likely the haircut. Hair is (as you've possibly discovered) a medium that's more than a little tricky under the scissors. Many of us have attempted to even up our tresses ourselves and have looked like badly shorn sheep until we could get the hairdresser to rectify our amateur efforts. We suddenly have a newfound respect for the beautician who can whip our wild manes into some sort of acceptable, if not gorgeous, appearance. The haircut has become perfected through shared knowledge that was very slow in becoming accessible just a few years ago. The sophistication of hair textures, resilience, natural wave, and the myriads of hair products have made the near impossible at least manageable. The science of the haircut has rendered many of us less distressed over the tresses nature gave us. The experienced eye and hand of the stylist actually makes some of us deliriously happy with the creation. So you can be assured that as a hairstylist you would make a real difference in people's lives. We all need the services of a competent haircutter and if he or she can actualize the way we desire our hair to be, it not only improves our self confidence greatly, it affects everything else about us. We have even coined the expression that we are experiencing a "bad hair day." Your haircut can make or break you—it's become that important to our self images.

Very few of us can afford that $200 haircut, but it does tell us just what lengths we will go to have the best looks that nature and its most qualified aides can bestow.

HAIR COLORISTS

Aside from the haircut, the second most important attraction is to have great hair color. In the last few years it has become possible to have any tint or dye in choices that are expanding annually. The most recent hair colors are the vibrant blues and greens that are used on natural and synthetic hair. The colors actually vie with those of tropical birds, they are so vivid. Rock bands set the style of wild uncontrolled manes and crazy drop-dead neons. The trend has continued and expanded. There are many places that cater to these fashions and the hair dye manufacturers are keeping up with the demand. Many of us are happy to just be highlighted, rinsed, or dyed with a moderate amount of color to enhance nature's colors. There is also the middle road that is more daring and requires the rich deep hues that dyes now offer to alter their looks to simply dramatic! And finally the blonds, the most popular hair color change worldwide. More women bleach their hair than the total numbers of those who request dyes. Marilyn Monroe probably did more for the blond hair business than anyone else before or since. She obviously had bleached hair, and prior to her adoration as a film star, bleached hair was just not considered a society approved option. Only if you were a movie star of her caliber could you expect to sport bleached blond hair without people looking askance. Luckily for all of us there is little that we could imagine now that would not be acceptable as hair color.

The hair colorist is the highest paid per job technician in the beauty salon. Like a super hairstyle, terrific hair color is the domain of an artistic eye. There are thousands of clients out there who look like their hair was dyed or bleached. The hard part is to make someone look subtly more attractive with a better hair tone. For the millions of ladies who follow the old adage "only her hairdresser knows for sure," it is still a personal matter whether they add color to their hair or not. They would just as soon have their audience think that they were born with their choice of color.

A SHOW OF HANDS

One of the most influenced areas for specialization is manicuring. With a massive influx of no-appointment, in-and-out-in-twenty-minutes nail salons, things got a bit out of control for the state cosmetology boards. While some manicurists were licensed, most were not, and when lawsuits ensued from all too common fungal infections carried at salon from client to client, new laws forced all operators to be licensed. Thus control was reestablished, and all manicurists were availed of the same education to prevent this and other diseases from harming the public and to make the profession more appealing. There was a short span of time where many potential clients were so fearful of these infections that they refused to let any licensed manicurists touch them and simply did their own nails as well as they could. There were many lawsuits in the New York area and other sections of the country. Shortly afterward, many states adapted by passing laws that clearly spelled out responsibilities to correct the problems. Many new positions and titles became available to those in the manicuring field. You could assume any one or more of the following posts: manicurist apprentice, manicurist instructor, manicurist manager, or manicurist. The other title of nail technician has also been used in certain states.

Nail technology schools opened en masse, adding and creating many new jobs within the manicuring profession. Nail specialists now are aware of safety and health standards as well as the cosmetic beauty of the well groomed and polished nails of the hands and feet. As a fashion accessory, the nails surely receive as much attention as does the hair. A well manicured set of nails are cared for weekly and you can see that the salary from this kind of client following could be quite dependable.

Men as well as women use the services of the manicurist, so if you prefer to cut, file, and buff rather than applying nail laquers, you may want to consider working in a barber salon on gentlemen's hands.

MAKEUP ENHANCERS

Not only the frame but the picture, also, should attract our attention. In bygone days, the fair of face really had little competition. Today, the hair, at least in Europe and America, has taken the lead. Facial care and its partner, makeup, are next in line for beauty enhancement. Although we rely on professionals to do our hair and we learn to cleanse our skins, apply emollients, and makeup, we are still on our own, so to speak, with our faces.

We, as a country, are beginning to take advantage of the services of the aestheticians. The cost of facial treatments are unfortunately prohibitive for the mainstream to take advantage of them. So if you opt to work in this category, you are quite well guaranteed of luxurious surroundings and of a compensatory salary. Most women and men who avail themselves of facial treatments and massages do so on a rather sporadic schedule, say once a month. Skin care specialists are very well paid and enjoy an unusually calm and serene atmosphere in which to work.

The makeup end of aesthetics is the fashion arena of ever changing looks. Again the creative challenge is present. In the last ten years, the makeup artist has come into his or her own. They are so highly paid for skilled work that they are hired per hour rather than per day even when doing demonstrations for the most well known cosmetic companies.

Makeup artists go "on location" for most of their work unless they are employed by a very busy salon that can attract enough clients to keep them fulfilled financially. The areas with the highest demand for really great makeup artists are New York City and Los Angeles. Many of the recognized artists work internationally on the sets of modeling shows, TV productions, and movie locations.

Being a makeup artist means that you will have to be a trendsetter, as the world of cosmetics at that level is always desirous of the "new" and more daring. Sometimes the person being made up needs to look very old, very sick, ghoulish, angelic, innocent, romantic, or weathered. Your job would be the challenge of any or all of these effects manifesting through pencils, brushes, and colors.

ELECTROLYSIS

Electrolysis is a technique that removes unwanted hair from all parts of the body. Most often it is facial hair that is removed by this process. Suppose that you have very thick, dark eyebrows. Although you have plucked them repeatedly, your eyebrows are still too heavy to allow your eyes to be seen to their best advantage. Electrolysis could permanently tweeze those thick brows away. Your face will look different every time you alter one of your characteristics. It is as wonderful and exciting to see these transformations as it is to see the pleasure that they instill.

RESEARCH

Laboratories provide challenging jobs for those interested in the chemical end of cosmetology. Products need to be formulated correctly so that people who use the cosmetics will benefit and not have an allergic reaction. Both the creation of new products and the improvement of standard products are the work of *chemists*. A college degree is required for this job.

The person who tests the formulas on the customer is a *product formulation tester*. His or her work consists of experimenting with the actual new product on the patron's hair or skin. These patrons do not pay for the work done since they are taking a small risk that they may not react well to the new product. But they usually receive very good hair and facial care because the licensed cosmetologist who does the testing has had the benefit of many years of experience before being advanced to the position of formulation tester.

MANAGEMENT

Career possibilities also lie in owning, managing, or instructing at a beauty school or salon. As long as you have the capital to invest, you can be a partner or an owner of a beauty salon or beauty school. There are laws in the various states that govern the amount of space required for a salon or school, and the size needed certainly affects the investment required.

Depending on the size of the school or salon, one person might both own and manage the business as well as work on hair. In larger salons where there are many employees, the manager sees to hiring, time schedules, and appointments. He or she sets up demonstrations and coordinates the entire working machinery of the salon. Obviously a well-managed, large salon with many patrons would bring larger responsibility and a higher salary.

COSMETOLOGY INSTRUCTORS

Possible career choices could also be sought in the teaching areas, which range from public to private establishments. With some of the latest laws and the expansion of certain specialities, instructors are more needed to cover the varied locations. You could instruct in a beauty school, a vocational high school, or perhaps a nail specialty school.

There are many exciting and challenging positions in teaching. You will be the one responsible for starting many a cosmetologist on their way. It is strictly the quality of the education that makes a good professional. Teaching does demand a whole different set of skills. Even if you were a well known artist in creating hairstyles or makeup, it doesn't mean that you have the attributes to be a skilled instructor. I have witnessed instructors short on patience and long on talent just take over, cut the model's hair, and leave a student wondering how the cut was accomplished. Remember that the student pays for the information and your job as teacher is to impart that knowledge with dignity.

USING COSMETOLOGY EDUCATION FOR OTHER CAREERS

The cosmetic chemist is the one responsible for creating all the cosmetic products used in the industry. A need is seen when a client requests a solution to a particular problem. Both an inquisitive and creative mind would be mandatory for this post. You would have to be knowledgeable in both chemistry and cosmetology to be a success in this area. What makes or breaks many a cosmetic company is the ability to create the product first and get ahead of the competition. And, after all, that is what most fashion industry related businesses have to do. Competition is always your toughest problem. The major interest of any of these companies is a fountain of youth in a tube, and all the products created year after year are full of that hope.

Maybe you have discovered since your graduation from beauty school that you have a strong affinity for sales. This talent could be used right in your current place of work if there are enough products for you to work with. It would be a matter of combining your ability to sell treatments and other beauty products along with your current profession in cosmetology. However, if you want to concentrate on the potentially large income that sales alone can afford, you might look into straight selling of any numbers of cosmetic products or equipment. Companies that produce hair, facial, and body products are always searching for knowledgeable people to promote their lines. With your background in cosmetology, you could be the perfect person to present a cosmetological product to companies, businesses, hair salons, spas, or directly to the public. Salespeople make excellent salaries along with commissions and bonuses. Selling is merely convincing your potential buyer that he or she needs your product and if you believe that you are selling a good product, your sincerity will come through.

Maybe you have a flair for writing and would like to combine your cosmetological know-how with a career in expressing yourself on paper. You could write articles for beauty publications, magazines, textbooks, or even your own beauty club or association. Journalism based on the practical knowledge that you could bring to your reader would be a specialized area. You could become a beauty editor or a writer of a column on the latest haircuts, styles, hair coloring, nail laquers, or even facials. The world of beauty is ever expanding, and it would be difficult to find a publication read by women that did not have a section on beauty. Some trade pamphlets need just the speciality that you have to offer. There are thousands of products that are written about in the cosmetology area from makeup to toe nail clippers. All of these need accompanying written matter for directions for use. This could be a unique speciality niche for you!

ENTREPRENEURIAL COSMETOLOGISTS

This is an area that has had much exciting new growth in the last ten years. The lifestyles of the successful businesswomen of the 1980s and 1990s have created special needs that have never before been addressed by the cosmetology industry. The long and hard hours of these working women have robbed them of their usual time for beauty services. To fill in the gap, many salons have rearranged their normal schedules to accommodate these armies of workers. The salons are required to work late hours and Sundays to allow for the free time of the client. They are also forced to have many services in one place so that the few hours available can be used most efficiently. Phones are placed at the patron's manicure tables, massages are given at the same time as pedicures and manicures. Four operators are often working on the same woman at one time. If one hour is free, hair, nails, and facial all have to be squeezed in somehow. Rapid drying nail polishes and time saving haircuts have become *de riguer*! Some of these once-upon-a-time beauty parlors are now day spas where you'd be hard pressed not to find any beauty service that you could imagine. Leg waxing, electrologists, aestheticians, makeup artists, and great hair stylists are all under one roof.

MOBILE UNITS

One of the latest indulgences of the very rich is a van full of hairdressers, nimble manicurists, and makeup artists who pamper the client every inch of the way to his or her destination. That's right! As you are bumping along on the Long Island Expressway, your toenails are being painted, your hair is being styled, and you step out of the van like Cinderella stepping out of her pumpkin coach. Pretty and well coiffed for any event. The fee for this elaborate experience is $250 and the in-transit care is two hours in length. Mobile units were not an entirely new idea but one clever hairstylist turned the van into a luxury event and is enjoying an extraordinarily lucrative scheme. This van taking clients to any resort area could bring the owners a whopping income.

CHAPTER 2

FINDING THE RIGHT SCHOOL AND GETTING YOUR LICENSE

The cosmetology industry is regulated by the individual states so that you are permitted to work only in the one where you currently are licensed. Some states do have reciprocal agreements with others wherein you could use your license in another state with certain stipulations. Regimentation being what it is, you may find little clauses that will permit you to continue working in another state by taking a small course or paying a fee for the consideration.

All states have very rigid codes that must be followed or you could be censured and find yourself unable to keep your license. Do make the effort to write or call the state board of cosmetology where you plan to attend beauty school and inform yourself. Know the legal aspects of that particular state. If you know that you are likely to relocate, obtain the second state's licensing rules right away to save time and costly mistakes in your choices of needed curriculum. All states stress different areas in your cosmetological studies. So if you are informed as to what will be needed where you will ultimately practice, you could save yourself time, money, and make a smoother transition.

It would be impossible to list every beauty school or to point out every advantage of getting your cosmetology education at one school or another. But we will try to cover several types of cosmetology educational offerings located in several states to give you an idea of what is generally available.

SCHOOL CATEGORIES

Public Schools

Schools offering beauty courses break down into three categories. The first of this group is the public school. Many schools offer cosmetology courses at an introductory level. In Florida, for example, high school students can enroll in cosmetology instruction in high schools, in area vocational-technical centers, and in community colleges.

Selecting an approved public cosmetology school can save you time and money. If you take cosmetology courses at a public school during your high school years, you can avoid the usual beauty school fees. In many high schools, students enter a beauty program in the eleventh grade for three hours every day. In the summer, they take training for six hours a day, and they take three hours a day of courses during the twelfth grade. In the vocational centers and community colleges, classroom time varies. If a student has completed all required subjects, he or she will attend classes for five to six hours a day. All postsecondary training is taught at a rate of five to six hours each day with the entire courses taking anywhere from 600 to 1,200 hours, as required by law. The individual school must certify that the student is ready for the exams.

Some states, such as Florida, have an extensive system of public cosmetology schools located in high schools, education centers, vocational centers, junior colleges, community colleges, adult programs, and adult centers. These technical facilities are scattered all over the state so they can be easily reached. Even the Florida School of the Deaf and Blind at St. Augustine offers cosmetology as a career.

There are eighty approved public cosmetology schools in Florida, if both day and evening schools are taken into consideration. Two of these are housed within correctional institutions.

California has many public schools where cosmetology is offered. A list of these qualified establishments may be obtained by writing to the California State Board of Cosmetology, in care of the California Department of Consumer Affairs. Part-time attendance at a school of cosmetology will meet California law requirements that everyone must attend a public school until their eighteenth birthday. After a person reaches that age, he or she can take cosmetology courses full time, and then be licensed. California has a new continuing education requirement.

California's public cosmetology programs are in colleges, vocational centers, high schools, junior colleges, occupational centers, and adult schools. There are thirty-one schools listen in the state's catalog.

Several other states also offer comprehensive cosmetology programs in their public school system. The junior year in high school seems the normal time to start these classes. If you are interested in taking cosmetology courses while you are still in high school, and your school does not offer any program, check with your local school administration for any possible classes in the area. Try to locate a school where you can take advantage of cosmetology instruction.

There are some schools that are neither strictly public nor private. You will pay a small amount of money for your education, but because of state funds within that particular school, your tuition will be much less than a private beauty school. These are considerations that you will want to take into account before you decide upon a school.

Private Schools

The second category of cosmetology schools is the private school. There are extensive differences in some of the schools due to instructors, standards of education required of the instructor, and the attitude and ability of the manager of the school. One very clever young lady revealed her technique for the best way to find the right school: Go to the best salons in town and ask their newest operators and apprentices where they took basic training. One way of judging the quality of a school's curriculum is to find out whether or not a school's graduates are getting jobs after graduation. After all, that is your primary concern. You may already know that a particular salon is your choice for work, so don't be shy about talking to its manager and finding out his or her preferences in cosmetology graduates. He or she will be glad to tell you. The manager is running a successful business and intends to keep up its standards by hiring well-instructed graduates.

Advanced Training

The last category of schools is the group that offers advanced training in cosmetology. This group is mentioned only briefly, as you may or may not elect to attend advanced training. In certain beauty salons, new techniques are demonstrated by permanent or traveling instructors. These new methods are shown to operators so that they can incorporate the current styles or trends that have just come into fashion. Fashion is constantly changing, and makeup and hairstyles must keep up with the latest "look." If you are an operator whose patrons demand the latest haircuts and styles, and your salon does not provide a periodic demonstrator, you will want to attend master classes to learn some fine points. In these classes, you will benefit from the experience and wisdom of a well-established professional hairstylist. It may be someone who is well known as a competition hair designer, a precision cutter, or a recognized colorist. Any added knowledge that you acquire will surely mean added clients and, of course, the compensatory salary and tips. These special schools may appear to be extremely expensive, but the $100 or more you pay for the day's class could mean a large difference in your income.

Choosing Your School

There are probably many beauty schools in your community, so make a list of all the ones that you might consider and call for an appointment. Try to sit in on a full day of work, instruction, and practice classes. If your area does not have a school that will let you sit in on classes, at least try to meet the classroom instructor and manager of the school. You will get a better idea of how the institution is run if you have the chance to communicate with the administrator directly. Remember that you are going to be paying to learn. By learning as much as you can about a school before you pay your tuition, you can help to guarantee that you will receive a good education. Fees vary widely depending on your locale, but you can expect to pay anywhere from $3,500 upward for the minimum hours of schooling. In New York City, it would not be unusual to pay over $6,500 for the school's required hours. But even with the best school, there is no guarantee that you will graduate. If you do not pass your state exams, you may have to return for more schooling at your own expense. So make a careful choice. Once you have committed yourself to the idea of becoming a cosmetologist, work hard and don't be discouraged if things seem to move at a snail's pace. Nothing is easy at the beginning, and every cosmetologist that I have spoken with admits that beauty school, like all schools, is a challenge. You will experience satisfaction and a feeling of accomplishment for many years after you have mastered your craft.

The years needed to complete your cosmetology schooling will vary according to how much time you are able to give your classes and practical assignments. If you attend full time, you could finish your schooling in as little as eight months. "Full time" would mean an eight-hour day, holidays excluded. If you attend only in the evenings, you would take about twice as long to complete the required hours. Of course, every state is different, and some require as many as 2,000 school hours, so you would finish in a little longer period of time. You might be going to classes as much as eight hours a day or as little as eight hours on Saturdays only. The less concentrated the time, the longer the course. Another curious thing that appears in some manuals is that a beauty school hour is only fifty-five minutes long. Be sure to ask about it so that both you and your faculty come out with the same total at the end.

Financial Aid

Financial aid is available in various states. As you might suspect, the aid is proportional to your own ability to pay. Aid can be obtained as a grant, which does not have to be repaid, or in the form of a loan that must be paid back. Most beauty schools have information about the types of financial assistance that you may be eligible for. Some of the financial assistance for which you may qualify are Basic Educational Opportunity Grants (BEOG), Supplementary Educational Opportunity Grants (SEOG), National Direct Student Loans (NDSL), and Guaranteed Student Loans (GSL). When you consider any cosmetology schools, these are the programs that you will want to investigate if you need assistance. Remember that these programs, too, may change; but as new titles and programs become available, you will learn of them only by being constantly in touch, asking questions, and keeping informed. Ask for brochures on the available programs so that you will be able to think them through clearly before you make any agreements to take a loan. Not all schools that teach cosmetology are qualified to give financial help. There are government regulations that dictate policy on giving money for tuition.

There are also agencies in the larger cities that try to help you find financial aid after you are enrolled. If you find yourself unable to keep up your tuition payments, it would be foolish not to take a loan, especially if you find yourself near to completing the required hours. To start over again at a later date would probably be extremely costly. Tuitions are constantly rising in the private cosmetology catalogs. But it is of paramount importance that you complete the minimum schooling at one time. Otherwise the critical knowledge you need for your state boards may be too dated or drawn out for you to remember.

APPRENTICESHIPS

After you have completed your state licensing, you may want to apprentice in a better salon. The purpose behind this is to develop as a good hairstylist and earn an excellent salary. If you desire to be associated with a salon with a reputation for high style or trendsetting, you must be prepared to accept very low compensation while you closely observe a well-established operator in that particular salon. You will be expected to put in normal working hours (usually an eight-hour day) and do everything that is asked of you by the busy top hairstylists. This could include shampooing, assisting with hair treatments, holding hair clips, and drying hair. You will not do haircutting or final styling until you have learned all the fine points of the specialized techniques. You could apprentice for as many as two to three years in a very elaborate salon. It all depends on your ability to learn to cut hair with dexterity and cleverness. There are specific haircuts and styles that better known salons have made famous. To learn a detailed type of cut is painstaking but absolutely necessary.

Apprentices Prior to Certification

Not all states have regulations that permit students to apprentice before securing a license. An apprentice is someone who learns by on-the-job training. The difference in this type of apprenticeship from the type just discussed is that this type of apprentice is clearly a trainee and has not yet accumulated the required educational hours to take the state boards. In some states where apprentices are schooled in beauty salons, state regulations will designate in every detail the registration requirements for the apprentice and the instructor-to-apprentice ratio in the place of business. In states that permit apprentices, strict laws stipulate all the conditions under which apprentices may be trained. These laws are clearly stated in the brochures put out by the specific state. If you are considering training as an apprentice prior to taking your state boards, it is imperative that you read all materials pertinent to registered apprentices. The fee paid by apprentices is not listed in most advertising brochures. Also, be sure to make inquiries at your local beauty salon to see where you actually would take all the needed courses. They may or may not be given in the same location.

Apprenticeships also vary in actual required hours from state to state. The average appears to be two years of noncertified, but registered, apprenticeship in a beauty salon under the tutelage of the designated number of certified operators. The required years of work would differ according to the individual's capabilities.

LICENSING REQUIREMENTS

Minimum Age and Schooling

The minimum age and amount of formal schooling required for licensure differ from state to state. So before you make plans to enroll in any cosmetology course be sure to find out the minimum age at which you can get a license. Some states don't even permit the state examinations until a particular age, so determine when you will be able to take the exam before you enroll. The average age for entry into cosmetology schools seems to be sixteen. Average schooling requirements vary much more widely. In Texas, for example, you can enroll in cosmetology school at the age of sixteen, and you need only have completed the seventh grade in elementary school. In Washington, D.C., you need only to have completed the eighth grade, but must be sixteen years old. So you can see that there is a variance in licensing requirements among the states.

Some states allow special testing for people who do not speak English well. If English is not your first language, investigate your state laws through a translator. Many states provide a practical test rather than a written test for those who do not speak English.

Application for Licensure

Once you have completed the required number of school hours for your state, you must apply to take the state board examinations. Your state has forms that are prescribed by the state cosmetology board. Every state has different time schedules to be followed, and you should check to see how far in advance you need to apply to take the exams at the designated time. You may find that application has to be made weeks or months in advance. So even if you have not yet graduated from beauty school, look into scheduling your exam.

There is also a fee, called the initial licensing fee, that must be paid to the state when you take your state boards. You will want to set that amount aside ahead of time.

When the time comes to actually obtain your license, inquire about renewal procedures. Your license is not a lifetime affair. It has to be renewed once every year in some states and once every two years in others. Most states have a set month wherein you are to renew cosmetology licenses. In New York, for instance, cosmetology licenses are renewed on July 1. Check with your state and any other where you may want to work in the future to learn about procedures. Because of large amounts of paperwork, state departments are always very slow, so licensing takes time. Be sure that you have proper licensing so that waiting to receive a license does not cost you working days.

Reciprocity between states means that if you are a licensed operator in one state, your training is recognized by many other states with similar cosmetology licensing rules and regulations. Wherever required hours and courses are alike, you probably will be able first to attain a temporary license from the new state, and then acquire a permanent license. Again, time will be of the essence. State departments are not intentionally trying to slow you down or prevent you from working, but you should allow several months in most states to receive all the necessary documents after you have made your initial application.

Licensing Examination

There is a National Cosmetology Examination now offered in thirty states. This test, consisting of one hundred questions, can be as long as one-and-a-half hours or as short as one hour. Records of the test are kept in the National Interstate Council of State Boards of Cosmetology.

There are special books now in print that will help you study either to pass the regular state boards in your state or the national examination. The books will help you to know what to expect in the exams and how to conduct yourself at the examination. They also give you sample questions to test your knowledge in all the areas that you are expected to understand. When you know what to expect and what types of questions will be asked, you will be much better prepared and less worried about either the written or the practical tests.

Ask at your local bookstore for the books; if they are not in stock, the bookstore can order them for you so you can brush up on all the work that you have covered in your cosmetology course.

CHAPTER 3

COSMETOLOGY CURRICULUM

We have seen a considerable amount of revision and new additions to the old cosmetology courses given in the schools. New laws have caused a more carefully defined curriculum as operators are made aware of possible pitfalls and health hazards to their clients. Chemicals used in cosmetology particularly are being more carefully addressed and new processes are specifically pointed out. The school of cosmetology is responsible for preparing students who are informed and who will be able to perform their work with care and pride, with absolutely minimal risk to any client.

SAMPLE CURRICULA

The following curriculum example clearly spells out new regulations that have recently occurred in the State of California, Board of Barbering and Cosmetology, Title 16, Division 9, Code of Regulations:

(a) The curriculum for students enrolled in a cosmetologist course shall consist of sixteen hundred (1,600) clock hours of technical instruction and practical operations covering all practices constituting the art of cosmetology pursuant to Section 7316 of the Barbering and Cosmetology Act.

(b) For the purpose of this section, technical instruction shall mean instruction by demonstration, lecture, classroom participation, or examination; practical operation shall mean the actual performance by the student of a complete service on another person or on a mannequin. Such technical instruction and practical operations shall include:

Subject	Minimum Hours of Technical Instruction	Minimum Practical Operation
1. *The Barbering and Cosmetology Act and the Board's Rules and Regulations*	20	
2. *Cosmetology Chemistry* (Shall include the chemical composition and purpose of cosmetic, nail, hair, and skin care preparations. Shall also include the elementary chemical makeup, chemical skin peels, physical and chemical changes of matter.)	20	
3. *Health and Safety/Hazardous Substances* (Shall include training in chemicals and health in establishments, material safety data sheets, protection from hazardous chemicals and preventing chemical injuries, health and safety laws and agencies, ergonomics, and communicable diseases, including the HIV/AIDS and Hepatitis B.)	20	
4. *Theory of Electricity in Cosmetology* (Shall include the nature of electrical current, principles of operating electrical devices, and the various safety precautions used when operating electrical equipment.)	5	
5. *Disinfection and Sanitation* (Shall include procedures to protect the health and safety of the consumer as well as the technician. The ten required minimum operations shall entail performing all necessary functions for disinfecting instruments and equipment as specified in Sections 979 and 980. Disinfection should be emphasized throughout the entire training period and must be performed before use of all instruments and equipment.)	20	10
6. *Bacteriology, Anatomy, and Physiology*	15	

Subject	Minimum Hours of Technical Instruction	Minimum Practical Operation
7. *Wet Hair Styling* (Shall include hair analysis, shampooing, fingerwaving, pin curling, and comb-outs.)	25	200

8. *Thermal Hair Styling* (Shall include hair analysis, straightening, waving, curling with hot combs and hot curling irons, and blower styling.)
   A. Thermal styling
   B. Press and curl
	20	40
		20

9. *Permanent Waving* (Shall include hair analysis, chemical and heat permanent waving.)	20	80
10. *Chemical Straightening* (Shall include hair analysis and the use of sodium hydroxide and other base solutions.)	20	25
11. *Haircutting* (Shall include hair analysis and the use of the razor, scissors, electric clippers, and thinning shears, for wet and dry cutting.)	20	80

12. *Haircoloring and Bleaching* (Shall include hair analysis, predisposition tests, safety precautions, formula mixing, tinting, bleaching, and the use of dye removers. Shall not include any credit for color rinses.)
   A. Haircoloring
   B. Bleaching
	40	50
		20

13. *Scalp and Hair Treatments* (Shall include hair and scalp analysis, scientific brushing, electric and manual scalp manipulation, and other hair treatments.)	5	20

Subject	Minimum Hours of Technical Instruction	Minimum Practical Operation
14. *Facials*		
A. Manual (Shall include cleansing, scientific manipulations, packs, and masks.)	5	10
B. Electrical (Shall include the use of electrical modalities, including dermal lights and electrical apparatus, for facials and skin care purposes; however, machines capable of producing an electrical current shall not be used to stimulate so as to contract, or for the purpose of contracting, the muscles of the body or face.)	10	15
C. Chemicals (Shall include chemical skin peels, packs, masks, and scrubs. Training shall emphasize that only the non-living, uppermost layers of facial skin, known as the epidermis, may be removed, and only for the purpose of beautification. All practical operations must be performed in accordance with Section 992 regarding skin peeling.)	10	15
15. *Eyebrow Arching and Hair Removal* (Shall include the use of wax, tweezers, electric or manual, and depilatories for the removal of superfluous hair.)	10	20
16. *Makeup* (Shall include skin analysis, complete and corrective makeup, lash and brow tinting, and the application of false eyelashes.)	15	10

Subject	Minimum Hours of Technical Instruction	Minimum Practical Operation
17. *Manicuring and Pedicuring*		
A. Water and oil manicure, including nail analysis, and hand and arm massage.	5	15
B. Complete pedicure, including nail analysis, and foot and ankle massage.	5	10
C. Artificial nails		
1. Acrylic: liquid and powder brush-ons	10	50 Nails
2. Artificial nail tips	10	50 Nails
3. Nail wraps and repairs	5	20 Nails

(c) The board recommends that schools provide training in the area of communication skills that includes professional ethics, salesmanship, decorum, record keeping, and client service record cards.

(d) No credit of any type shall be given for time spent in laundering towels or in washing or scrubbing floors, walls, woodwork, toilets, or windows.

NOTE: Authority cited: Sections 7312, 7362, and 7362.1(c), Business and Professions Code. Reference: Sections 7316(b), 7321(d)(1), 7362, 7362.5(b) and 7389, Business Professions Code.

A second example of a beauty school curriculum comes from a catalog advertisement. This particular cosmetology school is located in New York City. The classes represent what you could expect to learn there in eight months.

Course	Total Hours
1. Fingerwaving	200
2. Permanent Waving	175
3. Haircutting and Hairstyling	125
4. Dyes, Bleaches, and Rinses	100

5. Scalp Treatment 50
6. Shampoos 25
7. Manicuring 100
8. Facials 50
9. Sanitation, Sterilization, Hygiene, and Anatomy 50
10. Tests and Exams.. 25
11. Shop Management and Business Ethics... 50
12. Nondesignated Time 50

Total 1,000

After the completion of the diversified courses in the cosmetology curriculum, you may find yourself doing any or all of the various jobs in a beauty salon. Or you may want to specialize.

SPECIALIZED COURSES

In many states, if you hold a specialty certificate, you are permitted to work in only one particular field. The following definitions of specialties were taken from the *General Rules and Regulations* including the Cosmetology Commission Sanitary Rulings from the Texas Cosmetology Commission.

Cosmetologist—A cosmetologist (operator) license authorizes the holder to practice all phases of cosmetology in a beauty salon or any specialties in a specialty shop.

Wig Specialist—A wig specialist certificate authorizes the holder to practice wiggery, hairweaving, or perform eye tabbing in a beauty or specialty salon.

Manicurist—A person holding a manicurist license may perform for compensation only the practices of manicuring and pedicuring in a licensed beauty or specialty salon.

Shampoo conditioning specialist—A shampoo specialist certificate authorizes the holder to practice the art of shampooing, application of conditioners and rinses, scalp manipulation, and to sell shampooing hair goods in a licensed beauty or specialty salon.

Facial specialist—A facial specialist certificate authorizes the holder to practice facials, application of facial cosmetics, manipulations, eye tabbing, arches, lash and brow tints, and the temporary removal of facial hair in a licensed beauty or specialty salon.

Hairweaving specialist—A hairweaving specialist certificate authorizes the holder to practice the art of hairweaving in a licensed beauty or specialty salon.

There are many areas in which you may desire to specialize. As you can see from the certifications, you might be able to go directly into a special field with only a set curriculum for your specialty area. Or you may have to complete all the required hours in your state, take your state boards, and then specialize. In states with specialty certificates you cannot perform activities not designated by law. To do so might cause you to have your license revoked. Not all states allow specialty certification courses, but most states do have manicuring-only classes for certification.

LIMITED CERTIFICATES

In some states, you will discover that the license is called a limited certificate. A limited certificate is one that takes only a few school hours to complete. Anywhere between one hundred and three hundred hours could qualify you for a manicurist certificate, for example. A proportionate number of hours are designated to teach you all you need to know on that one topic.

Limited course offerings in cosmetology schools can qualify you to take the state boards in that one special field. Here is a school description of a manicurist course:

Course	Total Hours
1. Orientation	4
2. Manicure Tools and Use	9
3. Nail Structure (Theory)	1
4. Sterilization and Sanitation	2

5. Manicuring Procedure and Hand Massage 84
6. Manicuring Practices.. 7
7. Manicuring for Men 3
8. Tests 3

    Total 113

Remember also that in some states, there is no license requirement for manicurists, wig stylists, receptionists in beauty schools, and assistant manager positions.

SUPPLEMENTAL COURSES

There are supplementary courses offered in some states to give a wider scope to your original learning. These extensions are aimed at helping you develop additional talents in your own field. Suppose that you had gone to barbering school, had become very much in demand, and were offered a position to dress the hair and do the makeup for a traveling rock group. Since you are only licensed to style hair, that would limit your work, and the rock group requires that only one cosmetician travel with them. What you could do is quickly return to school. But this time you would take your barber's certification to a beauty school and take a shortened course.

Not every state has this type of arrangement, but it is a great convenience if it exists. The following is an example of one program designed for barbers who want to get their cosmetology licenses. The curriculum, excerpted from the California Code of Regulations, shows in detail what classes and hours would be needed to do a crossover from barbering to barbering/cosmetology licensure.

950.9. Curriculum for Cosmetology Crossover Course for Barbers

    (a) The curriculum for students enrolled in a cosmetology crossover course for barbers shall consist of a minimum of four hundred (400) clock hours of technical instruction and practical operations covering those cosmetological practices that are not a part of the required training or practice of a barber.

(b) For the purpose of this section, technical instruction shall mean instruction by demonstration, lecture, classroom participation, or examination; practical operation shall mean the actual performance by the student of a complete service on another person or on a mannequin. Such instruction shall include:

Subject	Minimum Hours of Technical Instruction	Minimum Practical Operations
1. *The Barbering and Cosmetology Act and the Board's Rules and Regulations*	10	
2. *Cosmetology Chemistry* (Shall include the chemical composition and purpose of cosmetic, nail, hair, and skin care preparations. Shall also include the elementary chemical makeup, chemical skin peels, physical and chemical changes of matter.)	5	
3. *Health and Safety/Hazardous Substances* (Shall include training in chemical and health in establishments, material safety data sheets, protection from hazardous chemicals and preventing chemical injuries, health and safety laws and agencies, ergonomics, and communicable diseases, including HIV/AIDS and Hepatitis B.)	20	
4. *Theory of Electricity in Cosmetology* (Shall include the nature of electrical current, principles of operating electrical devices, and the various safety precautions used when operating electrical equipment.)	5	
5. *Disinfection and Sanitation* (Shall include procedures to protect the health and safety of the consumer as well as the technician. The ten required minimum operations shall entail performing all necessary functions for disinfecting instruments and equipment as		

Subject	Minimum Hours of Technical Instruction	Minimum Practical Operations
specified in Sections 979 and 980. Disinfection should be emphasized throughout the entire training period and must be performed before use of all instruments and equipment.)	10	10
6. *Bacteriology, Anatomy, and Physiology*	5	
7. *Wet Hair Styling* (Shall include hair analysis, shampooing, fingerwaving, pin curling, and comb-outs.)	10	35
8. *Thermal Hair Styling* (Shall include hair analysis, straightening, waving, curling with hot combs and hot curling irons.)	5	15
9. *Permanent Waving* (Shall include hair analysis, sectioning patterns, chemical and heat permanent waving.)	10	35
10. *Chemical Straightening* (Shall include hair analysis and the use of sodium hydroxide and other base solutions.)	5	10
11. *Haircutting* (Shall include hair analysis, basic guideline and sectioning, the use of the razor, scissors for wet and dry cutting.)	2	10
12. *Haircoloring and Bleaching* (Shall include hair analysis, predisposition tests, safety precautions, formula mixing, tinting, bleaching, and the use of dye removers. Shall not include any credit for color rinses.)		
A. *Haircoloring*	20	15
B. *Bleaching*		5
13. *Scalp and Hair Treatments* (Shall include hair analysis, scientific brushing.)	2	5

Subject	Minimum Hours of Technical Instruction	Minimum Practical Operations

14. *Facials*
  A. Manual
    (Shall include cleansing, scientific manipulations, packs, and masks.)
	2	5

B. Electrical (Shall include the use of electrical modalities, including dermal lights and electrical apparatus for facials and skin care purposes.)	7	5
C. Chemicals (Shall include chemical skin peels, packs, masks, and scrubs. Training shall emphasize that only the non-living, uppermost layers of facial skin, known as the epidermis, may be removed, and only for the purpose of beautification. All practical operations must be performed in accordance with Section 992 regarding skin peeling.)	10	15
15. *Eyebrow Arching and Hair Removal* (Shall include the use of wax, tweezers, electric or manual, and depilatories for the removal of superfluous hair.)	5	5
16. *Makeup* (Shall include skin analysis, complete and corrective makeup, lash and brow tinting, and the application of false eyelashes.)	5	10
17. *Manicuring and Pedicuring* A. Water and oil manicure, including nail analysis, and hand and arm massage.	5	15
B. Complete pedicure, including nail analysis, and foot and ankle massage.	1	3

Subject	Minimum Hours of Technical Instruction	Minimum Practical Operations
C. Artificial nails		
1. Acrylic: liquid and powder brush-ons	5	10 Nails
2. Artificial nail tips	3	10 Nails
3. Nail wraps and repairs	2	5 Nails

(c) The board recommends that schools provide training in the area of communication skills that includes professional ethics, salesmanship, decorum, record keeping, and client service record cards.

(d) No credit of any type shall be given for time spent in laundering towels or in washing and scrubbing floors, walls, woodwork, toilets, or windows.

Being human, we are all subject to changing our minds, and the cosmetological courses of study are now ready to deal with such problems with equanimity. So if you find yourself unhappy in the area of your current career or even your years of preparation, there are solutions that don't make you start from the beginning. The following is from the *Board of Barbering and Cosmetology's New Regulations,* California Code of Regulations.

950.10. Credit for Special License and Transfer of Training

(a) A student transferring from one course of study to another, or a holder of a special license (e.g., manicurist or aesthetician) who enrolls in a general course of study (e.g., cosmetology), shall receive credit for total clock hours completed and credit for and a balance of the minimum hours of technical instruction and the minimum practical operations required in each applicable subject as follows;

1. *Total Clock Hours Credit*

A. Cosmetologist course to aesthetician course. A student transferring from the cosmetologist course to the aesthetician course shall receive a credit of 35 percent of the total clock hours earned while enrolled in the cosmetologist course.

B. Cosmetologist course to manicurist course. A student transferring from the cosmetologist course to the manicurist course shall receive a credit of 20 percent of the total clock hours earned while enrolled in the cosmetologist course.

C. Aesthetician course to cosmetologist course. A student transferring from the aesthetician course to the cosmetologist course shall receive a credit of 65 percent of the total clock hours earned while enrolled in the aesthetician course. A holder of an aesthetician license enrolling in the cosmetologist course shall receive a credit of 65 percent of the total clock hours required for the aesthetician course.

D. Manicurist course to cosmetologist course. A student transferring from the manicurist course to the cosmetologist course shall receive a credit of 70 percent of the total clock hours earned while enrolled in the manicurist course. A holder of a manicurist license enrolling in the cosmetologist course shall receive a credit of 70 percent of the total clock hours required for the manicurist course.

2. *Credit and Balance for the Minimum Hours of Technical Instruction and Minimum Practical Operations Required*

A student transferring from one course of study to another, or a holder of a special license who enrolls in a general course of study, shall receive a credit and balance for the minimum hours of technical instruction and minimum practical operations required by subtracting the number of hours and operations earned by the student or licensee while enrolled in the prior course from the minimum hours of technical instruction and minimum practical operations required for the new course in each applicable subject. If the student has earned more hours or operations in the prior course than are required in a specific subject of the new course, then that student's balance of hours and operations required in that subject shall be zero.

(b) Credit for a special course shall not be given to a student in the cosmetologist course until completion of the number of hours of instruction and training in a school of cosmetology which, when added to the number of hours for which the student is entitled to credit for the special course, will equal the minimum number of hours required for completion of the cosmetologist course.

(c) Training received as an apprentice shall not be credited toward a course of training in a school. Training received in a school shall not be credited toward training in an apprenticeship program.

NOTE: Authority cited: Section 7312, Business of Professions Code. Reference: Section 7367, Business of Professions Code.

TRAINING FOR INSTRUCTORS

Another whole area of specialization involves the instruction or teaching fields. There are many positions open to instructors, demonstrators, and even lecturers in the cosmetology field. Some states require special education courses for these posts while others demand only a license in cosmetology from that state and several years of experience as a practical cosmetician. If you are interested in a teaching job, the best way to find out the details is to write your state's board of education and find out the current prerequisites. The department can also supply you with the list of all public and private schools of cosmetology where you will be qualified to instruct. Be sure to find out when your license expires and keep it up-to-date. You need to hold a cosmetology license to teach. If you find that your license has expired, you could waste a great deal of time getting it back again.

MANAGERIAL AND BUSINESS POSITIONS

Managerial posts may interest you. There are many of these jobs in department store and beauty salons, specialty shops, beauty shops, facial schools, facial salons, cosmetology schools, electrology schools, wiggeries, and cosmetic businesses.

Last, but not least, your specialty may be in the business end of the cosmetology world. You may want to own a chain of shops or salons. Although this is not likely to be an immediate accomplishment, you may want to start with owning one beauty salon as soon as possible. It is really quite common to see several salons owned by the same proprietor. Some people have very good business minds. You could combine your talents as a cosmetician and your competitive abilities by owning your own beauty school or salon.

CHAPTER 4

NAIL TECHNICIANS

The nail industry has grown so fast within the last several years that there are now new laws as well as new positions in the field. This once tedious service has been taken over by efficiency-oriented young people, working in beauty parlors and independent nail salons. They work with such speed and deftness that it is not unusual to be in and out of a nail salon with a complete manicure and pedicure in half an hour.

Unlike operators in nail salons, operators in beauty salons rarely have appointments scheduled throughout the day. However, beauty salon manicurists and pedicurists have the potential to earn good tips because beauty salons generally charge more for their services, and clients are appreciative of the more luxurious treatments they receive in the beauty salons. The nail salon is geared to efficiency first, but both methods have their following.

The pay for an operator is directly proportional to that individual's agility with the implements and ability to apply artificial tips, wraps, and polish. Around the New York City area, an operator's income can be as high as $75 to $140 per day, including tips.

LICENSING AND TRAINING

We can look at the examples of a few states to see how the rapid—some say *too* rapid—growth of the industry has brought about new laws and positions. Maine, for example, has a manicurist apprentice license available that requires the operator-in-training to be under the direct supervision of a licensed individual in a licensed shop. In most states a set number of school hours must be taken to qualify for the nail technician's license. The hours vary from 100 to 500 state by state. These lessons are to be taken in a licensed cosmetology or licensed nail school. The cost for this schooling varies from school to school, but runs from around $1,300 to $2,400.

The license for a manicurist manager is offered in two states. This position would entail authorizing only cosmetic care of nails. Minnesota requires an additional 2,700 hours of schooling beyond the manicurist's license to fulfill this position.

The nail technician instructor could be employed in either a nail school or a cosmetology school. The specialty has grown so rapidly over the past few years that the demand for manicurists alone without hairdressing skills has made a vast market in itself. A nail technician instructor fills this post by having been a licensed nail technician first and then completing instructor training which is around 350 to 1,000 hours of schooling. After passing the instructor practical exam you would be permitted to teach nail care only. A salary of about $800 to $1,000 per week would be the expected wage for the position in and around New York City.

The nail salon manager, or for that matter any person with a license in manicuring, could well own his or her own nail salon. These can be extraordinarily successful as there is minimal expense for equipment. A few manicure tables and a small, clean, and well-lighted salon are the basic requirements. Your operators usually take home half of their fees plus their tips. You would have half of all the income and any monies you yourself made doing manicures as well. Nail salons are one of the best examples of ultra-successful small businesses. It would be difficult to find an urban city block that doesn't have either a beauty or a nail salon.

The most radical and immediate change we have seen in the nail care industry in the last few years has been the advent of viral, fungal, and bacterial infections. Along with the incredible growth of the industry came the discovery that these infections can be easily spread from one client to another by using the same implements on many customers. Cut cuticles are an easy source of entry for these infections and recuperation can take many months. At times, lawsuits have resulted. State health boards are taking a closer look at the nail industry, and new laws have been passed that require individual kits for personal use by each patron. In New York state, emery boards, chamois buffers, credo knives, and pumice stones are either prohibited or must be used on the same patron only. Many salons have provided personal emery boards, orange sticks, and a kit or envelope to hold them.

Expenses incurred in complying with these new laws are certainly substantial for many nail salons and beauty parlors. Some salons have asked customers to purchase their own kits and save them the added expense. Under the new laws, the manicurists are to be fined for noncompliance if disinfecting machines and antiseptics are not up to the new standards.

MANICURING

Many people who have had serious nail problems have discovered that with consistent professional care, nails can become strong, healthy, and attractive. It may be that the nail's being incorrectly filed has caused the weakness and breakage.

You will notice after several trips to the manicurist that the routine is a very exacting one. A professional manicurist trains the nail to grow in a certain manner to strengthen it and to make the nail more attractive to the eye. The end of the nail can be treated so that breakage is kept at a minimum.

One of the advantages of being a manicurist is that your work will not demand that you be on your feet, like other cosmetologists. Instead you can be comfortably seated. Your arms rest on a manicure table, and even when you administer hand and arm massage to a patron, you work gently with no great expenditure of energy. If standing on your feet all day as a hairdresser is too exhausting for you, you might consider specializing in manicuring.

In a busy salon, a manicurist is kept working most of the time. Your tips will depend on your clientele, but the more customers that return to you on a weekly basis, the better your salary will be.

PEDICURING

If you choose to do manicuring only, there is normally enough demand in any beauty or nail salon to keep you busy. But unless you work in a large salon, you will not be able to survive doing just pedicures. Most women who are on their feet for a good portion of the day appreciate the services of a pedicurist. The punishment that feet endure is somewhat counterbalanced by the pedicurist. When toenails are properly clipped, trimmed, filed, and buffed, shoes fit better and blisters are less likely to occur. When toenails are too long, serious damage can occur to the whole foot. People develop incorrect patterns of walking when nails that are too long force feet back and do not allow them to lie flat. It is imperative that the length of toenails be watched, the width of the nail be guided in its growth pattern, and corns, if present, be kept under control. A pedicure is not a luxury. Good nail care is truly a necessity.

After their nails are filed and smooth, some people may want to have them painted. In the summer, or anytime that toes are visible, colored nail polish is a fashion accessory.

SALARIES AND WORKING CONDITIONS

As a manicurist, your weekly salary could be any amount depending upon creative talents and your own ability to attract customers. You will have to advise your clients how to protect their nails by wrapping them, how to strengthen the vulnerable ends of long nails, and how a complete plastic nail can shield a badly broken nail until it has a chance to grow out. A manicurist who merely cleans, trims, and polishes nails will earn much less than one who is competent in creatively reconstructing nails.

In New York City, a manicurist may earn as much as $650 a week, plus tips. A pedicurist, who, by the way, makes a higher per-client income, may earn from $18 per hour upward.

You will be able to find work in beauty salons, department stores, barber shops, hotel beauty shops, and specialty salons for nails. There are many new openings yearly for manicurists and pedicurists. It is a profession that takes care, patience, and a genuine interest in a client's well-being.

CHAPTER 5

POSITIONS FOR COSMETOLOGISTS

The most exciting thing about seeking work in the field of cosmetology is that your choices are so many. Need and imagination have created dozens of new avenues for you to explore. The variation on the original job which was most often hairdressing in a beauty shop has become so multifaceted that you can customize your career. From part time work where you might apply nail extensions to a full time career catering to the rich and famous at spas or aboard luxurious cruise ships to owning a beauty publication of your own, it's all within the realm of a career in cosmetology. Many operators wear several hats in that they are hair stylists several days a week and then do on-the-set hairdos for fashion models for a shoot or prepare a person's hairstyle for a television appearance. If you select any of the myriad specialities of the industry, you can create an area for yourself. There is also a good bit of mobility within the industry itself. If you start out in one particular area, it is not written in stone that you need make it your life career. You could make a change by apprenticing to someone very recognized in the business for a small salary or no salary at all. The advanced learning and association with that person's name is as much of a bona fide credential as possible. Many famous hairstylists had the patience and foresight to apprentice as their first job.

Your ambition will guide your ultimate goal, but the first position you take after you are licensed will set the tone toward that end. If you are limited as to time and financial restraints your decision will of course be affected, but you should be aware your possibilities are many and that your dreams of success can be realized if you look at each job as a stepping stone toward your final post.

CHOOSING A PLACE TO WORK

You will want to seek employment as a cosmetologist in the most favorable area for your own needs, be they financial, aesthetic, or both. Your cosmetology placement service can help you decide where to apply and will guide you to openings available. Though no one has a crystal ball to predict the future, you must try to foresee the potential for continued success with patrons, both as you begin your job and after you have expanded your clientele. It would be unwise to take a position in an area where you know that a competitor at a more desirable location would be opening soon.

After you get your state certificate, you may want to place your own "position wanted" ad in your local paper and in any city where you might want to work.

Make phone calls to any of the beauty salons, hotels, department stores, or specialty shops where you think that you might like to work. Set up appointments for interviews, and be sure to look neat and well-groomed when you go to the interview.

Beauty Shops

Most jobs in the field of cosmetology are in beauty salons. These salons can be situated anywhere, from the local shopping mall to elegant specialty shops. There are many jobs for general operators and specialists alike. The general employment rate in cosmetology currently seems to be a two-to-one ratio—there are usually two cosmetologists for every one job that is open. So scout your potential area for possible job availability, and allow for time to find a good position. To have the job you desire, you may have to commute a little. Not all cosmetologists are working, or even desire to do so. Statistics are based both on how many cosmetologists are licensed in a particular state and on how many currently are employed in that state. There are always jobs available in service careers, and cosmetology, like all other services, is growing rapidly in certain high-income areas such as New York, Los Angeles, San Francisco, Atlanta, and Chicago. But finding employment can be extremely difficult in areas of lower incomes.

Day Spas

The day spa is the latest innovation to give full cosmetological services all under one roof and in quick and yet luxurious ways. A client could have a manicure, pedicure, facial, and a massage all at the same time. This isn't everyone's ideal but the day spa has become the saving grace of the horrendously short-of-time woman executive–mother–homemaker. Her time is such that all of her beauty needs have to be met in perhaps an hour. The availability of many specialists to work simultaneously eliminates her need to run from salon to salon for leg waxing, electrolysis on her facial hair, nail extensions, haircut, style, and dying, and perhaps a massage. There was one salon in New York City that did all of these services many years ago, so this is not a new idea, but certainly a timely one. There are several day spas around and the advantages for the operators are weighed in the fact that they could have many clients in the ordinary time that they luxuriously saw one. Not everyone likes to work in a hurry, so if that particularly appeals to you, this could be a good area for investigation. Not all the clients who avail themselves of day spas are pressed for time, but many are and you would be expected to accommodate the patron's specific needs.

Children's Salons

If you really love working with children, there are wonderful positions open for shampooing and cutting children's hair. Many department stores have special shops to cut children's hair in surroundings oriented to their particular needs. In working with children, patience is a must. Many children hate having their hair cut. Even if you try every trick in the world, from hobby horse chair seats to bribes of balloons, it can still be a challenge. But it can pay very well, and parents are grateful.

Nursing Homes

There are many places where you can be employed. If you like service work, you may want to work in a hospital or senior citizen's home, giving cosmetic services to elderly or incapacitated people. Your rebody. Sanitary codes strictly dictate cleanliness. Your training in beauty school will have shown you how to follow these codes.

Cosmetic companies usually place help wanted ads, but if you have decided to go into facial work, contact one of the companies directly. You can call or write for an appointment. Tell them about your interests, qualifications, and experience, as well as your schooling and licenses or certifications. Have a well written, attractive résumé to leave with the personnel interviewer. There are many assistantships in large companies, and working as an assistant could be a way for you to reach your final goal.

Barber Shops and Men's Hair Salons

Barber–hairstylists find work in barber shops, unisex shops, hotels, department stores, and specialty shops. There are many small businesses that cut men's hair. A visit to inquire about future employment may be your best course. There are barbers who work on men, women, and even children. Your work as a unisex stylist would permit you to practice anywhere that a cosmetology license is not required.

As a specialist in any area, such as coloring, wiggery, shampooing, or hairweaving, you are limited to working in those salons that offer the particular specialty that you are qualified to practice.

CHAPTER 6

BEAUTY SALON EMPLOYMENT

A visit to a beauty salon tells you just how many persons it takes to run that form of business with efficiency. Positions have become more and more specialized and as a result the numbers of people who work in cosmetology have increased. The beauty salon hires as many operators and unlicensed persons as are needed to attract clients. Some salons need the talents of one type of technician only, such as a fast haircut shop, while others hire the full complement of every variety of hairstylist, colorist, nail specialist, facialist, barber/stylist, salespeople and makeup artist.

The numbers of people who were employed as cosmetologists and related workers in 1992 were listed as 676,000. The projection for this same group for 2005 is 915,00. Nearly half of this number who are currently working are self-employed. It is an area of tremendous job opportunity and there is no occupation with a brighter future. The unemployment rate is and has been very low for all recorded years.

While new and innovative specialties keep appearing in this field, and they always will due to its connection with fashion, there will be more and more position openings in many places. The latest specialty is hair braiding and it is being incorporated into every level of beauty shop, be it the one-chair shop or the gigantic salon. As fashion trends set the pace, the beauty salon's job is to avail clients of any new service next to immediately. Many customers still arrive at the beauty salon with the latest magazine photographs and request that particular hairstyle. If the operator cannot replicate it, you may not see that client again as she'll go where the latest fashion can be attained.

Serious damage could occur to the hair if the dye is left on too long. Hair colorists earn the highest salaries, anywhere from $600 per week upward, plus tips, depending on their particular place of business.

Permanent waving, hair pressing, and chemical hair relaxing are all specialties. The size of the salon and the volume of business will dictate how many of these professionals are employed in a salon. Any specialist is able to command a salary of at least $600 to $750 a week. Again, it depends on whether or not he or she is paid a straight salary, a commission, or a combination of the two. Tips are usually excellent in any good hair salon, and the more specialized the service, the higher the tips.

Manicurists

Manicurists and pedicurists also have their places of employment in beauty salons. Patrons sometimes have these services done while their hair is being dried. Pedicurists normally work in a sectioned-off area to give the patron more privacy. In larger salons these services are well rewarded with tips. Salaries vary from a per-patron percentage to a straight salary of around $250 a week. This is not a clear-cut area, as many manicurists earn a salary that changes, sometimes from week to week. It seems to depend on regular patrons who come back time and again.

Makeup and Facial Specialists

Makeup artists and facial experts might be employed in a beauty salon, probably a very large place of business offering full services to the patrons. Services in this type of establishment would include leg waxing, wig styling, and even salespeople demonstrating products to patrons.

Hairstylists

The most important and most recognized people in any beauty salon are hairstylists. These men and women are highly skilled and well-trained experts in cutting hair in particular hairstyles. Haircutting is the most difficult part of handling hair. Hair can have different textures such as wiry, slippery, thick, fine, coarse, limp, and curly. Hair is a challenge to control, and haircuts train hair to lie in a desired manner. Top stylists can and do earn salaries commensurate with their abilities. Haircuts alone in New York can cost up to $100. The average hairstylist there earns about $40 per cut, plus tips. Arrangements vary from employer to employer. If you are working for yourself, the sky is the limit for your potential income, as you do not give half to an employer.

Other Positions

There are other positions in the beauty salon that do not require state licensing. These jobs entail handling supplies. Stockpersons and laundry and cleaning personnel are all necessary for a functioning shop. The person who sees to the smooth running of it all is the manager. This person is responsible for the coordination of hiring and firing. He or she also makes up the employee work schedules, schedules vacations, orders paychecks and uniforms, places advertisements, orders supplies and sales merchandise, and acts as peacemaker should any disagreements arise in the shop. A manager's thorough knowledge of beauty professions and the business workings of the salon can guarantee the success of the shop. A manager's salary normally corresponds to his or her responsibilities. If the salon is particularly large and complex, the salary will be excellent.

Retail Sales

Retail selling in beauty salons has become a way to add to the income of the shop itself and to the incomes of the operators, manicurists, pedicurist, and wig stylist.

Most of the more famous salons promote their own cosmetic and hair products. Depending on how large the retail aspect of their business is, many salons actually have a salesperson in the employ of the salon. If there is no specific salesperson, the operator who recommends the special hair treatment or shampoo will receive commission on the sale. The beauty salon, of course, covers its cost and a small commission as well. Many specialists sell almost all of the creams, lotions, packs, scrubs, astringents, cleansers, and makeup that they use in the salon itself. Once the client is introduced to the product and is given instruction on how to apply it, he or she can do the same service at home. A shampoo specialist usually recommends the type of shampoo and rinse needed for a customer's particular scalp, and more often than not, these products are sold in the beauty shop. Product lines have been expanded to include the salon's own hairdryers, combs, styling brushes, and even bags large enough to carry all the products.

Manicuring specialties and different products used to make the nails stronger and keep them from looking unkempt are also sold in beauty salons. These creams are applied daily to supplement the once-a-week visit to the manicurist.

Wigs and postiches are often sold in beauty salons as well as all the required accessories, such as wig spray, carrier cases, brushes, and even clips and bows. These items can increase the income of the salon tremendously. And if a salon services wigs and postiches, it would be a mistake not to sell them. The profit is very high on both natural and synthetic pieces.

Most women and men who have just come from a hairstylist's care and look their best will assume that part of the result is the product the hairstylist used. The psychology of selling the product right there is very powerful. If you suggest to your client that she or he go out and purchase the items that you have used in their treatment, chances are small that they will even remember the name of the product, let alone the procedure. Having the products accessible is only good business and good treatment for your client. Many salon patrons feel that it was not their weekly visit to the hairstylist that was expensive but all those irresistible little goodies that added up to a very sizable income for the salon owner.

CHAPTER 7

AESTHETICIANS AND FACIALISTS

We have seen a tremendous increase in this area of cosmetology due to women travellers who now demand that the American salons keep up with their international counterparts. The facial was the least utilized of the beauty services for it was thought to be purely cosmetic, but is now recognized for its therapeutic values. Asian and European women as well as men have treasured their facial skin and have raised the facial to a near-scientific level. Americans have long been known for their fascination with hair and makeup, so the advent of the facial salon did not make waves for many years. Now it is commonplace to have complete offerings—from herbal to electrical appliance facials. People with a public image to maintain have known the wonderful benefits to be gained from facial deep pore cleansing to relaxing facial massage. Facials have always fallen in the category of definite pampering as they are relaxing and feel luxurious, but the truth is that your facial skin needs more than soap and water to battle the foul air that we live in. Many a movie star credits her flawless skin to her facialist and considers those visits to be just as critical as any other cosmetological one. It is interesting to note that just a few years ago there were a handful of skin care salons that basically used all their own skin products exclusively. Now you could find a facialist in almost any major hair salon or beauty parlor or department store salon. The demand for total beauty care has forced the bigger salons to include aestheticians (also spelled as estheticians) among their offerings. If a salon has a small but sophisticated following it would not be uncommon to find the manicurist or makeup artist doing facial work, which could be a consideration as a career choice.

The facial has a following among younger people as well. There are many teenagers who have problem skin and are helped greatly by thorough skin cleansing that is only done by professionals with the knowledge and experience of dealing with their skin difficulties. Skin care has come into its own with the increase in facial salons by nearly tenfold just in the city of New York alone, and that's in the last seven years. Expansion has caused much specialization within the area.

THE NEED FOR FACIAL SPECIALISTS

Too much of any natural element can guarantee a skin of leather consistency. Exposed skin will form a heavy and darker texture to protect itself from further damage. The sad thing about damaged skin is that the damage is more often than not permanent. Skin dried out from too much sun will never be soft and delicate again. We are still learning what permanent damage the sun can cause. We now know that a little direct sunlight is vital, but it must be acquired gradually. If our faces were not exposed, we would not need highly specialized techniques to protect this vulnerable area. Grime and dirt attack our faces and hands. But even hands have tougher skin than faces. Not only that, but gloves and mittens at least partially protect hands during many times of the year. So what appears to be one of the most delicate of skin areas is expected to meet all kinds of weather and remain attractive, young, and as unlined as possible.

There are many ways moisture can be retained in the skin, facial muscles toned and exercised, and dirt and excessive oil removed from the face. The specialist who is most knowledgeable in this field will not only have a cosmetologist's license but will have had several weeks of intensive schooling in highly skilled techniques.

Even if a person is not troubled with any particular skin problems and has the luck to have absolutely radiant skin, the services of a skin specialist can ward off potential trouble through skin analysis, helping the skin to stay as young as physically possible.

Skin care is also known as *aesthetics.* If someone specializes in the care of the skin, he or she could be known as a cosmetician, a skin care analyst, an aesthetician, a skin therapist, or a skin specialist. When you are looking for work, you could conceivably be listed as any of these and still work exclusively with the face.

There are several ways to break into the facial care world. But first you will have to complete your state boards so that you will be a licensed cosmetologist. In some states you will go directly into facial specialty work without further instruction. Some states require that you obtain a specialty certificate. In New York, for example, you need both the certificate and the state license to land a good job with higher pay and more opportunity for advancement. But you can get a job doing facials in a beauty salon with just your state licensing. In general, if you want to specialize, try to get as much instruction as you can afford from as highly recognized an authority as possible. Education is the fastest and surest way up the professional ladder. One word of recommendation from a well-known figure in your chosen field can be extremely valuable.

EDUCATION FOR FACIAL SPECIALISTS

Your basic skin care work will be covered in beauty school training. You will learn how to manually cleanse, manipulate, and massage the skin. You will have a little skin analysis, some anatomy and physiology pertaining to the skin, and a brief course on diseases of the skin. It is critical that you understand all the possible disorders of the skin for health precautions. You should also know your own limitations in being able to determine whether a minor case of acne can be corrected or whether a doctor's advice is needed. You must be able to identify a bump or lump on or beneath the skin's surface before you apply anything to the client's skin. It could be a harmless fatty cyst or something infectious that could be contagious to you or other patrons.

You will want to familiarize yourself with the skin's functions and conditions so you will be able to advise your client on preventive or corrective measures. Most clients will have similar problems. Many younger people have skin that tends to be too oily, and middle-aged, too dry. It is pleasurable to have the skin manipulated at any age, and a variety of massages are indicated by skin types. Some massage is for relaxing and some is for stimulating. The muscles of the face benefit from the effects of massage. Tensions and stress show on the face more than on any other part of the body. Massage can reduce stressful feelings by causing tension to disappear. Tight muscles can also be therapeutically relaxed with heat and light. Some techniques employ several processes in one treatment. You might have electric massage (stimulation) with heat, or after an application of an abrasive cream, steam might be prescribed. Chemical reactions speed up with the addition of heat. If the opposite treatment is called for, astringents cool and close pores. A skilled skin specialist can teach you how to take the best care of your skin. Cleaning your type of skin can be more complex than just soap and water, and many soaps dry delicate facial skin. Even if you have plenty of oil now, you could be harming your skin by not giving it the proper care it needs.

FINDING A SCHOOL AND A JOB

Scientific skin care is now available in most large cities and in many smaller ones. As it is a comparatively new career field in the United States, you may have a little difficulty locating a school that specializes in facial care. Look under "schools" in your Yellow Pages. If you do not find any listing, write to your state board requesting information on specialty schools. You might try calling a major city telephone operator for a skin care school listing.

Most states require 300 to 900 hours for licensure. Some states also require a high school education before you can enroll in a skin care school. The approximate cost for tuition in such a school in New York City is nearly $6,000 for 600 hours. This would be a complete program for makeup techniques, facial procedures, body waxing, and would lead to a New York State Esthetics License. There are private schools (like the one just mentioned) where your costs are the highest, but remember that these courses are also offered in some public high schools where you could be looking at virtually no cash outlay.

One particular school has branches in many large cities across the United States. The woman who manages the New York branch says that no one had even heard of this specialty where she came from in England. So if facial care seems like an interesting career possibility to you, do not be discouraged by its apparent inaccessibility. Facial schools do exist in the major cities, and you should be able to find one by checking the Yellow Pages.

Seventeen states have made a distinction between a cosmetology license and a facial care or aesthetician's license. Upon completion of an average of 600 hours of schooling in facial care you could be a fully qualified specialist in these states. You would still have to pass your exams but not the extended ones set up by the cosmetology boards. Your work would be restricted to facial care and makeup.

In California there is a special course of 600 hours that permits you to apply for certification and registration as a cosmetician/aesthetician. Like a skin care or facial specialist, you are permitted to give facials; apply makeup; give skin care; remove hair by depilatory, waxing, or tweezing; and apply false eyelashes. You are licensed to apply preparations to the neck, bust, arms, and upper body. Massaging and cleaning skin by machine and manually are also services you are permitted to perform. To become a cosmetician in California, you must be seventeen years of age, have completed the tenth grade, and received the minimum 600 hours of training from an approved cosmetology school. A cosmetician is prohibited from practicing any services beyond those mentioned in this paragraph.

Due to the limited number of strictly facial salons, there seems to be no problem in placing certified graduates. Salons contact the school in New York for recommendations, and the manager of this school believes that all of the graduates find work. About 250 students graduate each year. Incomes start at about $200 per week, plus commissions, or a straight salary of about $250. Commission comes from volume of customers or products sold to the customer. Facial salons often carry their own line of cleansing products and cosmetics.

OPENING A FACIAL SALON

After a student completes the facial care course, he or she often opens a salon. If you start with your own salon, the beginning may be a bit rough until you have established your own clientele. It is a very lucrative business that can be run by a small staff until you have more patrons.

If you open a skin care salon, you will then need a state license for cosmetology and a certificate for skin care. If you open a salon that dispenses only cosmetics and you demonstrate them, you no longer need a license in New York state. Check all laws before opening a salon, because laws are constantly changing. New state boards make new laws, and what was pertinent last year may or may not hold true this year. If you open a facial salon in Louisiana or Massachusetts, you will need only the facial course and no license from the state. If all this seems terribly complicated, it is because there are no national standards. Each state governs its own cosmetology businesses. It is not likely that you will practice in many states during your lifetime, but if you do move around, the sad truth is that you will have to take a practical and a written test every time you cross over a state line.

TEACHING FACIAL SPECIALTY SKILLS

Facial specialists may also find jobs as instructors in schools teaching facial care. If you are interested in teaching facial technique in New York state, you are required to have three years of experience in the field and the required teaching courses offered at the college level. A separate teaching license must be obtained from the state at a cost of about $500. Ohio requires 500 hours of schooling and a current license for managing cosmetologist or aesthetician. Check the requirements carefully in the state where you plan to follow a teaching career.

CHAPTER 8

MAKEUP ARTISTS

Do you have an artistic flair and a desire to create special effects? If so, you may be very well rewarded as a makeup person. The ability to use color to cause a particular visual image is highly regarded today. Most people know if they like what they see but they do not know what made this occur. The French have long understood the importance of fooling the eye and named this art form *trompe l'oeil*. A recent book by a truly gifted and internationally known makeup artist shows one model after another that has been dramatically transformed. Years are taken away, and what was rather mundane is nearly exotic after he has applied his masterful techniques. Makeup used to be very much of a try-and-try-again endeavor. If you got it anywhere near improvement, it was more by chance than talent. Now the age of the professional makeup artist is here. What was the realm of the fashion industry and movie sets is now available to the public at large. As you may already know, individual lessons or a professional application of makeup for an occasion that demands it can be very expensive. But more and more clients are demanding perfection and that means lots more positions will be available for makeup artists.

There was a very competent saleswoman/makeup artist employed by one of the major cosmetic companies who really understood color, shading, texture, and dramatic effect. She was immediately recognized for the talent that she is and is no longer selling eyeshadows, but creating faces for those who are willing and able to pay her hefty $150 to look great. The makeup artists most in demand are clever enough to capitalize on their talents and instead of simply coloring one face, they give instruction to groups at anywhere from $90 to $250 per person, depending on where they are located.

A big speciality of the recognized makeup artist is wedding parties. In the New York area, it would not be unusual to pay several hundred dollars for the talents of a known artist for just one face!

Makeup artists are highly recognized today as respected professionals in the beauty industry. The demand has shifted from making up actors and actresses to demonstrating to the public how to correctly apply the thousands of cosmetic products that confront the baffled purchaser in every department store in the world. With plastic surgery, a whole new aspect of makeup has emerged, and the makeup artist has dozens of clever tricks and illusions to communicate to the client.

The first responsibility that a makeup specialist has to his or her patrons is to analyze their skin and advise them how to clean it correctly. Everyone has a different skin type, and the balance between the skin's natural oils and what is applied externally is important. If you have skin that lacks moisture and oils, you will follow a program designed to save the resources that are already in scarce supply in your body. If your skin is very oily, it is unlikely that all areas of your face are in that condition. So a specialist's analysis is a form of advice to the patron, and the specialist must know the signs of dry or oily areas. When a specialist sees flakes of dry skin around a client's nose, for example, he or she should realize that those dead skin cells need to be removed so that the underlying cells can breathe. Contrary to belief, dry skin that is flaking does not indicate lack of oils, but the opposite. Stimulation to that area is needed so that dead cells are naturally sloughed off.

SKIN CARE

Makeup is a profession in which communication is vital. It is important for makeup specialists to clearly explain what problems they recognize in a customer's skin and how a beauty program is to be followed for best results. There are many people with beautiful faces now whose skin was not so trouble-free when they used improper care. Cleansing the face is a top priority. Cleansers come in liquid, cream, and even bar shapes. A combination of several of these cleansers is usually used to achieve really clean skin. Someone who lives in a city has more dirt to battle and needs more help in deep cleaning. Scrubs and pore cleansers are a necessity for normal or oily skin. Dry skin needs protection from the elements as well, usually in the form of remoisturizers.

Astringents are applied to every skin type to close pores. All preparations come in varying strengths, and your job will include understanding every type of skin's needs.

Unfortunately, the cleansing procedure removes needed oils as well as surface oil and dirt. Astringents also remove remaining surface oil, and this must be replaced by applying moisturizers. There are various ways to remoisturize the skin. The most delicate, the lightest creams, are the most easily accepted by the skin. Even if a person has a good supply of natural oils, there will be areas depleted of oils. Your professional eye will have to quickly analyze any problems and advise the patron of the most efficient way to deal with them. Your ability to save patrons time in their daily cleansing routine is very important. If they have to allot more time than is practical in their daily routine, they may not complete it. If so, the skin will suffer. If an individual takes preventions when he or she is young, he or she can maintain young, healthy, supple skin well past middle age.

COLOR

The amount of color in a face also can be changed with makeup. There are two ways in which color can work to improve appearance. The first is by altering the contour of the bones of the face. Every face is unequal in its two halves. Your job would be to see what is uneven and shade or add color as the fault dictates. One of the highest paid cosmetic models today has a notoriously uneven face. A breakdown of her features actually showed the two halves of her face to be unequal by an inch and a half. Most faces have much more subtle inequalities. This model supposedly was given a choice modeling contract because ordinary people could relate to her imperfect beauty and were more inclined to buy the company's cosmetics.

The second way in which color can be used to correct facial defects is in concealing certain "bad colors." If dark circles, sallowness, or ruddiness dominate a face, careful selection of concealers and foundations

LICENSING

Cosmetology boards for makeup are a requirement in many states. In most states, a small number of school hours are set aside for the strict pursuit of skin analysis, corrective or complete makeup, or application of false eyelashes. You will notice that all of these require actually touching the patron, the point on which laws differ. In some states, you cannot touch the patron without a license, and in other states, as long as the service is performed only on the skin's surface (makeup, electrology), a license is not required. There is no consistency in the states' prohibitions. Certain services that are considered purely cosmetic in some states are regulated by medical boards in others.

New laws are currently requiring licensure for all makeup artists in New York state. Other states may also redefine their laws as well due to more stringent regulations. There was news coverage recently about an unlicensed makeup artist in Washington D.C. who had prepared the mayor for a television show. The embarrassment could have been avoided if the artist had only been licensed!

When you are in department stores or other places where makeup is being sold you can quite easily pick out the licensed operator by the sole factor of whether or not she is actually touching the client. She is permitted to demonstrate on herself or describe the product's uses alone if she does not have legal licensure. You can see just how limiting this can be. A good makeup artist wants to paint a person's face and without licensing would be forbidden to touch or apply anything to a customer.

JOBS IN MAKEUP

The places where you might seek employment after you are a makeup person could be almost anywhere. Department stores, drugstores, cosmetic company demonstrations on various locations, beauty salons, specialty shops, promotionals, beauty shows, modeling shows, theaters, television, and movies all offer jobs for makeup specialists. Most jobs available are in the sales area of cosmetic companies. This is often the springboard for many career jobs in cosmetics.

The qualifications for finding a job in makeup include finger dexterity, patience, a good eye for facial structure, a clear understanding of colors and how to create them (remember that skin has its own color—it is not a clean white canvas), and a genuine interest in helping people to look better.

Pay scales vary greatly depending on which position you take. But starting pay is almost never below $250 a week. In large cities, pay would more than likely be over $300. Your decision to work on commission and salary or just salary will affect your income, too.

Makeup is a rapidly expanding field, and hundreds of jobs occur with each new cosmetic company. You have a wide open field from which to choose. You may select full- or part-time work, sales, demonstration, or even door-to-door sales. There is an opening in the cosmetic job market that could very likely satisfy you.

Makeup work has continued to be an area of immense growth. There is hardly any area in the world today where you cannot find diversified cosmetics from many companies. In New York City alone, millions of dollars are spent annually on cosmetic products. And thousands of jobs are created from this demand.

Makeup jobs are not found only in large cities. New products are distributed in the most remote corners of the earth. And as these products are distributed, they create jobs.

CHAPTER 9

ELECTROLOGISTS

The permanent removal of hair by electrical processes is becoming a much used service due to its ultimate timesaving and neatness. There are so many areas of the body that are covered with unwanted hair such as the upper lip, arms, legs, personal areas, and even hair line. When the hours and expenses are added up on the gels, depilatories, disposable razors, and waxing services it often makes more sense to seek a once and for all solution. The process is a little uncomfortable for the client but is good for a lifetime! It is definitely the age of time-saving, and electrolysis is the paramount technique of choice. There are many places where you could find the services of epilationists and thermologists—in day spas, beauty salons, or in specialty boutiques of their own.

Thermolysis (the most frequently used method of electrology) was found to be so efficient by those who took advantage of its benefits that the number of salons offering it in the New York area alone has increased from a few to several dozens in a decade. Many facial salons offer this service because the public has been made so aware of improved methods to remove unwanted hair. Pumice stones were the original hair removers, then crude salves, then razors, and finally hot waxes or depilatories. None of the aforementioned are permanent though, and as men who shave daily know very well, it takes time and careful attention to do the job.

The removal of unwanted hair is done by an electrologist or an epilationist. The actual procedure is called electrolysis, which involves permanently removing hair by removing the hair follicle with an electrical current. You may want to make an appointment with a professional operator if you think that you may be interested in a career in this area of cosmetology. The schools that teach electrolysis are quite frequently run by salespeople who sell the electrical equipment that is used in this process. Some beauty schools do teach electrology, but since there is no licensing required in many states, there are few schools that offer the course in their curriculum.

Our society dictates who should have hair growth, where it should grow, and even how much hair is socially acceptable. Long underarm hair with sleeveless clothing is not considered proper grooming in most social circles. Even nostril hair is groomed with scissors by a barber. You cannot have electrolysis on nostril hairs or hairs that grow on moles and warts. Your electrologist can advise you on other areas not suitable for electrolysis. If you are diabetic or have a pacemaker, it is advisable to have medical clearance before you have electrolysis.

As an electrologist, you learn how to insert a very fine needle or wire into a hair follicle. The needle (contrary to popular belief) never punctures the skin. It is merely inserted in the natural opening of the hair follicle. A gentle electrical current is then applied to the papilla (hair cell). As a result of this process, the papilla dies and the hair is then removed with a tweezer. An electrologist works with a large magnifying glass that has a light around its circumference. There is a certain amount of eye strain in this job because electrologists must concentrate on one hair at a time. After you build up your finger dexterity, you will be able to remove many hairs in a few minutes. The needle is held in one hand while you spread or stretch the skin gently with the other hand. While looking through the magnifying glass, you will be able to quickly guide the needle into the hair follicle.

EDUCATION

Electrolysis is generally considered to be the safest method of permanent hair removal if performed by a qualified electrologist with up-to-date electric equipment. Therefore it is critical that you attend a good school of electrolysis. In the state of New York, you will need to attend classes to receive your certificate. The typical school requires 120 hours of work. The curriculum consists of lectures, actual clinic work with electrolysis machines and patrons, and testing. The minimum age is usually eighteen, with no formal schooling required. There is usually no language barrier problem, as the work is of a practical nature. For instance, if you could speak no French and your patrons spoke only French, you would still be permitted to perform electrolysis on them. The only problem might be quoting fees or explaining the actual process if the patron wants to know how electrolysis works. But strictly speaking, you would not have to talk to the patron, only serve him or her. The current price of tuition at a school of electrology is around $1,250 for fifteen eight-hour days. There are evening courses and part-time courses, but you could conceivably have your certificate after three weeks of concentrated schooling.

LICENSING

Laws on electrology differ greatly from state to state. In Massachusetts, for example, 1,100 hours are required prior to taking a state board exam in order to practice electrolysis. In California, an electrology course of 500 hours taught by an established cosmetology or electrology school must be completed before you can apply for state registration and licensure. Also, the age limit is seventeen, and a twelfth-grade education is a prerequisite for taking the course. So you can see laws are drastically different in the field of electrolysis. In New York you could actually be setting up your own practice in a month's time, while in Massachusetts you would still be a student after eight months. You will want to consider the time needed to complete a course before you enter a program. You also must realize that if you do decide to take a course in New York and then move to a state with more stringent education requirements, you may find that you have to go back to school again.

FINDING A JOB

When you graduate from electrology school, you will be able to find work in certain specialty shops, department stores, or your own private salon, if you want to set one up. Unlike the other career possibilities I have discussed (with the possible exception of facial and skin care work), electrologists most often work for themselves. The equipment is minimal. A short wave machine, a couch or a hydraulic chair, and something comfortable for the operator to sit on, magnifying lamps, needles and needle sterilizer, tweezers, and a few antiseptic lotions will be all you need. At a cost of under $6,000 you could be in business for yourself! This is obviously a perfect job for someone who wants to be his or her own boss. Your time is your own, and the average hourly charge for electrolysis can be anywhere from $40 to $100 depending on your area of the country.

Insurance costs for an independent electrologist in New York state are about $125 annually. This fee is so reasonable because there seem to be few malpractice suits.

The field of electrology is wide open for earning. Large numbers of electrologists are not available, and the procedure of removing hair electrically is very time consuming. There are therefore plenty of job opportunities in this necessary and rewarding field. There are many people who have never heard of electrology, and with a little advertising and word-of-mouth praise from your patrons, you might easily establish a career for yourself in a very short time.

To help you learn more about electrolysis, there are several nonprofit organizations exclusively for electrologists. These groups are dedicated to the betterment of the profession, and most actively practicing electrologists are members.

One last word about the actual process of electrically removing hair. It is not painful, but because people have different tolerance levels, some people feel a slight discomfort in more sensitive areas, such as the upper lip. Legs are probably the least sensitive. Patrons who have been treated are usually extremely pleased. Facial hair can make a woman feel far less than feminine, and after all, the main purpose of all cosmetics is to make you your most attractive self.

CHAPTER 10

WIGS, HAIRPIECES, AND HAIR ENHANCEMENT

This is an area of cosmetology that has seen tremendous development in recent years. As all-out vanity and self indulgence increases, more and more people are demanding a way to replace their lost tresses. Men as well as women are looking toward buying hair in the forms of wigs, add-ons, wiglets, postiches, toupees, switches, falls, and hair extensions. Hair can be surgically replaced as well, but often is recognized by the sparse growth and visible scalp, punctuated at quarter inch intervals. The preferred methods are most often cosmetological. In my research I have even come across new methods of attaching a toupee by snaps! Small metal attachments are recessed into the scalp and the hairpiece is then snapped on or off as need dictates.

Hair extension is becoming extraordinarily popular, and given the current rates, a specialty in this area would guarantee an income in the range of $150,000 to $200,000 a year. It would have the potential of becoming intriguing work as well due to the many visible clients you could be servicing. Exclusivity in hair extension procedures would mean that you would do the monthly maintenance on the add-on. This is another area of solid income as the upkeep for each client would be around $35 to $50 per visit. Hair extensions grow along with your own hair to which they are attached and thus need more specialized care than your own natural hair.

There are many people who have suffered hair loss as a result of illness, hormone imbalances, and, more commonly, genetic traits. There are perhaps as many reasons to replace lost hair as there are methods.

Baldness would not be rectifiable by hair extension as there is no hair to extend, but options are many and your client can be helped by your informed advice.

CHOOSING A WIG

There are two kinds of hair available for wigs, natural and synthetic. A natural wig made of real human hair is the first choice. Human hair used in wigs and hairpieces is chemically boiled to removed the color. Then it is dyed to match a color wheel that gives a precise choice to the patron. Each wig or hairpiece if referred to by a certain number on the color wheel.

The wig must be carefully fitted to the patron's head. If it is too large, it can actually be shrunk by applying hot or warm water to the cap and leaving it to dry on a block smaller than the patron's head. Tucks also can be taken in the cap of the wig to make it the correct size. A new kind of wig has strips of hair held together by elastic. This wig is lighter and lets air reach the scalp because the hair is not a solid mass, unlike the traditional style.

The other kind of wig is made of synthetic hair. This type of wig has its limitations, and synthetic hair often is used in less expensive wigs. Modacrylic fibers are supposedly so cleverly used now that synthetic wigs can look very natural. Of course the actual construction of the wig itself can dictate the quality of the wig. Hand-tied wigs are the best quality, while machine-made ones are less desirable. Some wigs are made using both methods and are considered to be serviceable as well as ornamental. The hand-tied European wig is the most expensive, and the machine-stitched, synthetic fiber wig is the least expensive.

The cost of cleaning the two types relates to the original cost of the wig. The less expensive synthetic wig can be washed in ordinary shampoo and rinsed in water. The natural hair wig is cleaned in a fluid similar to dry cleaning fluid. This fluid is dangerous and must be used in a ventilated area.

Because the care of natural hair wigs is so extensive, the cost is much higher than for a synthetic wig. The natural hair must be conditioned, as natural oils must be cleaned out of the wig along with dirt. Gentle care will guarantee a long life to a real hair wig. It can even be dyed, unlike the synthetic wig.

Hairpieces come in varying sizes and lengths. Women use them for special effects, to give more height or weight to their own hair, or to fill in sparse areas. Hairpieces can be made of artificial or natural hair, machine made, or hand tied.

WORKING AS A WIG STYLIST

The job of the wig stylist is to fit, clean, cut, style, and comb out wigs and hairpieces. Packaging the wig in a carrier may also be a duty, as many women never come to the wig stylist, and the stylist must pack and send the wig back to the customer.

If a wig stylist works in a beauty salon, he or she may need a license as a cosmetologist. Often a wig specialist certificate is adequate to work on wigs in salons, department stores, specialty shops, or costume departments. State health codes set strict standards for wig handlers. No wig is permitted to touch another wig, and all wigs must be handled so that they are not contaminated by anything that touches them. The block that the wig rests on, the pins that hold it, and the rollers, clips, brushes, or combs that may come in contact with it must all be carefully sanitized.

Wig styling is covered in the New York state licensing for cosmetologists. This permits the wig stylist to actually work on the wig or hairpiece while it is on the patron. Not all wig stylists need to touch the patron, and each stylist has to decide whether he or she needs that extra licensing. If a person is merely selling wigs in a department store, it is highly unlikely that any certification would be required in any state, though he or she may wish to combine actual hairpiece work and wig styling. The particular question of who must be licensed for wig work seems to be undecided. The answer seems to depend on who a stylist is working for, where he or she is working, and if he or she has to touch the client.

SALARIES

Pay scale in the field of wig styling varies. A wig specialist usually receives a commission from the salon for each wig, plus tips. If you work only on the wig and never see the customer, tips would obviously not amount to much. If you are running your own wiggery where you are personally measuring the patron, acquiring, selecting, or recommending wigs (or even making them), and fitting, cutting, and servicing, then your income could be quite substantial.

Your actual salary would also depend greatly on where you are working. People in certain areas of the country find wigs more acceptable and more a necessity than in others. Large cities are where you would sell and service the greatest number of wigs and hairpieces. Most show business and theater personalities need wigs and own several postiches, toupees, or full wigs.

SELLING HAIRPIECES TO MEN

Men use hairpieces as much or even more than women. In large cities, there are full-page advertisements for hairpieces for men who are balding. Toupees are mentioned briefly here, as they are similar to, but not quite the equivalent of, the postiche for a woman, and you may or may not need licensing in your particular state to handle toupees. It all depends on the laws that cover your state's barbering codes and if hairpieces are regulated under your state's law. In New York City, licensing is needed, as measurements for wigs require touching the patron, the deciding factor. Men's hairpieces are not regulated by cosmetology boards. So though it is highly unlikely that if you work as a cosmetologist you would be doing men's hairpieces, you might be employed in a unisex salon where the question may arise. It is your job to be able to advise your patron, and you should be able to recommend a reliable men's hair care professional.

Hairweaving is performed on as many men as women clients. A customer should be advised of all possibilities before investing in either type of hair replacement.

CHAPTER 11

BEAUTY SALON OWNERSHIP

Owning a beauty salon may or may not be a goal of your cosmetological career. It goes without saying that many salon owners are not cosmetologists and that they are business persons only. In fact the statistics would appear to indicate that owning your own salon is not as common as it was ten years ago. The expenses today could well be a delineating factor and for some operators the freedom from having to always keep abreast of the economy is a big consideration. If you own your own beauty salon, you have the opportunity to make greater financial gains, but if things do not go well, you will then be the one to address all the losses. Even the most successful beauty salons have at times been forced to reduce their fees to clients due to slumps in general economy. The fluctuation of client fees for services tells you how well the beauty salon is doing in today's market. All of us need the services of hairdressers, and when you notice a price reduction in a haircut or a colorist's fees you are made aware of an astute business move being made and know that good managerial talents are looking after the survivalship of the salon. These would be just a few of your concerns as a beauty salon owner.

Current statistics show that one third of the working licensed cosmetologists (about 250,000 operators) own and work in their own salons. The greatest number of these are hairstylists. These statistics still indicate that advancement in the field of cosmetology involves owning your own salon. The obvious attraction is that you will be your own boss and you will reap more of the profits. Drawbacks are financial responsibilities if the business does not succeed.

Salon owners can earn a salary of between $25,000 and $100,000 annually, depending upon the salon's location and the number of steady clients.

When you are enrolled in cosmetology school, it is very possible that you will have several hours of instruction in owning and managing a beauty salon. In New York state, about 50 hours are devoted to this area in the private beauty school curriculum. Astute planning is of the utmost importance as many complications can develop in trying to coordinate a project of this size. The tiniest salon with an area to service two patrons at a time will have all the major problems of a larger one. The difference will be the dispersal of responsibility among the larger staff in a bigger salon.

Before you start your salon, check all the state codes and local laws that regulate owning and running your own salon. You will be responsible for everything, even if you do have a manager and a very competent staff. Ultimately, as the owner, you are responsible to the state and, of course, to all of your salon's patrons, whether you actually work on the person or one of your employees does. You will be responsible for insurance coverage, rental payments, salaries, hiring, firing, accounting, paying taxes on the business, and purchasing all the supplies. If you do not want to handle the day-to-day operations of your salon, you can delegate these jobs to a manager–operator who is qualified to manage a salon. This person should have many years of experience as a licensed cosmetologist and must be qualified for a managerial position. It is very difficult to run an entire operation without responsible help to rely on. A good manager is critical to the life of a well-run salon. Last, but surely not least, the personality of the manager can make or break your beauty parlor. A pleasant, attractive, well-groomed, intelligent, warm, and efficient person can coordinate the entire business, making it a pleasant place for workers and patrons alike.

STATE REGULATIONS

Every state spells out in detail how a beauty salon should be set up and how it should function. In Washington D.C., for example, the Cosmetological Act stipulates:

It shall be unlawful for any person to practice cosmetology for pay in any place other than a registered beauty shop: Provided, That a registered operator may in an emergency furnish cosmetological treatments to persons in the permanent or temporary residences of such persons by appointment. Every beauty shop shall have a manager, who shall have immediate charge and supervision over the operators practicing cosmetology.

Licenses have to be obtained for cosmetology salons, too. The following described how to proceed in the state of California in accordance with the regulations set forth by the California Department of Consumer Affairs. (Section numbers refer to specific code items.)

Establishment Defined

7346. An establishment is any premises, building or part of a building where any activity licensed under this chapter is practiced.

Application for Licensure

7347. Any person, firm or corporation desiring to operate an establishment shall make an application to the board for a license accompanied by the fee prescribed by this chapter. The application shall be required whether the person, firm, or corporation is operating a new establishment or obtaining ownership of an existing establishment. If the applicant is obtaining ownership of an existing establishment, the board may establish the fee in an amount less than the fee prescribed by this chapter. The applicant, if an individual, or each officer, director, and partner, if the applicant is other than an individual, shall not have committed acts or crimes which are grounds for denial of licensure in effect at the time the new application is submitted pursuant to Section 480. A license issued pursuant to this section shall authorize the operation of the establishment only at the location for which the license is issued. Operation of the establishment at any other location shall be unlawful unless a license for the new location has been obtained upon compliance with this section, applicable to the issuance of a license in the first instance.

Licensee in Charge

7348. An establishment shall at all times be in the charge of a licensee of the board except an apprentice.

Employing Unlicensed Persons

7349.   It is unlawful for any person, firm or corporation to hire, employ, or allow to be employed, or permit to work, in or about an establishment, any person who performs or practices any occupation regulated under this chapter and is not duly licensed by the board, except that a licensed cosmetology establishment may utilize a student extern, as described in Section 7395.1.

Any person violating this section is subject to citation and fine pursuant to Section 7406 and is also guilty of a misdemeanor.

Barber Pole

7349.   It is an unfair business practice to any person, firm, or corporation who engages in a practice regulated under this chapter to use the traditional symbol known as the barber pole, which comprises a striped vertical cylinder with a ball on top, with the intent to mislead the public in any manner that would make the public believe that barbering was being practiced in, or that a licensed barber is employed in, an establishment that does not employ licensed barbers.

Prohibited Uses

7350.   No person having charge of an establishment, whether as an owner or an employee, shall permit any room or part thereof in which any occupation regulated under this chapter is conducted or practiced to used for residential purposes or for any other purpose that would tend to make the room unsanitary, unhealthy, or unsafe, or endanger the health and safety of the consuming public.

An establishment shall have a direct entrance separate and distinct from any entrance in connection with private quarters.

A violation of this section is a misdemeanor.

Public Toilet Room

7351.   Every establishment shall provide at least one public toilet room located on or near the premises for its patrons. Any toilet room installed on or after July 1, 1992, shall be not less that 18 square feet in area. The entrance to the room shall be effectively screened so that no toilet compartment is visible from any workroom. The room shall be kept in a clean condition and in good repair, well lighted and ventilated to the outside air, and effectively screened against insects and free from rodents. The floor shall be of concrete, tile laid in cement, vitrified brick, or other nonabsorbent material. All sewer drains shall be connected to an approved disposal system, and shall be properly trapped. No restroom shall be used for storage.

Handwashing Facilities

7352. Every establishment shall provide adequate and convenient handwashing facilities, including running water, soap and approved sanitary towels.

Inspections

7353. Within 90 days after issuance of the establishment license, the board or its agents or assistants shall inspect the establishment for compliance with the applicable requirements of this chapter and the applicable rules and regulations of the board adopted pursuant to this chapter. Each establishment shall be inspected at least annually for compliance with applicable laws relating to the public health and safety and the conduct and operation of establishments.

OTHER REGULATIONS

After you have complied with the state codes, be careful to read all the local codes as well to be certain that you are not in violation. Careless misdemeanors can be costly.

Hairdressing and cosmetology rulings from the Department of State, Division of Licensing Services, Albany, New York, stipulates:

All beauty parlors shall be maintained and operated in accordance with the provisions of the State Sanitary Code, except in the City of New York where the New York City Health Code shall apply, and all licensees or persons employed or engaged therein or in connection therein shall comply with the provisions of such codes.

The New York City Health Code then proceeds to detail the amount, type, and correct usage of all equipment.

10.10 Water supply. An adequate supply of hot and cold water from municipal or satisfactory private source shall be provided for service for customers, cleanliness of employees, and for washing floors, walls, ceiling and equipment.

10.11 Waste Disposal. Waster water from all plumbing fixtures shall be discharged into municipal sewers where available. Otherwise suitable facilities shall be installed for the absorption of the wastes by the soil in the underground systems, so that no nuisance is created.

10.12 Plumbing fixtures. Plumbing fixtures shall be of impervious material and a type which is readily cleanable. They shall be free from cracks and from parts which are not readily accessible for cleaning. They shall be of a type which does not constitute a hazard to a public water supply through back siphonage.

10.13 Floors. Floors shall be of such construction as to be easily cleaned and shall be kept clean and in good repair. If carpeting or similar material is used for floor covering, it shall be of light color with a single loop pile of not more than one-quarter inch in height. Such floor covering shall be kept clean by vacuuming at least daily and shampooing at least annually and more frequently if the covering is not clean.

10.14 Lighting and ventilation. Lighting fixtures shall be in sufficient number and properly placed so as to provide adequate illumination. The shop shall be properly and adequately ventilated.

10.15 Cabinets. Cabinets shall be provided for storage of clean linen and towels. They shall have tight fitting doors that shall be kept closed to protect the linen and towels from dust and dirt.

10.17 Refuse. Covered containers for hair droppings, paper and other waste material shall be provided and maintained so that they are not offensive.

Though some of the stipulations are simple common sense, others are elaborately detailed requirements that you must follow to the letter when you open your salon. An unfavorable inspection could prevent you from opening if you are not within the code.

FINDING A LOCATION

After you have carefully established what constitutes a cosmetology business, you will want to familiarize yourself with the location and building floor plan you have chosen for your beauty salon. The first thing to consider is finding a good location where you will not be in direct competition with another beauty salon. Even with a large following you will need to have favorable conditions to succeed in your own business. Next you should ask if the place is large enough for expansion, or whether you will have to consider moving in a few years. Will it be convenient to your clientele if you do move after you are once established? Could you possibly afford to open another salon to accommodate a prosperous business? Will this be a convenient place for your staff to reach? You cannot possibly foresee all the "ifs." But a little foresight could help you decide on the location of your place of business.

When you invest in equipment for your salon, be certain that it is the best quality, because repairs of inferior plumbing and other equipment will cost many times more than if you had paid for good equipment at the beginning.

HIRING A STAFF AND GETTING STARTED

Once the final decision to own your own salon has started to become a reality, you will have to hire a congenial staff with professional knowledge and assets that will attract customers to your salon. Word-of-mouth is always the best advertisement, so you will want to employ hairstylists with good followings who will expand your business. It will be critical to your new salon to have some established clientele. Starting from the beginning and building a clientele is possible, but if prospective patrons see that you are busy with at least a few customers, their confidence will bring them to you more quickly.

You will have to decide the cost of your services, another "make-or-break" factor. Your operators deserve to be paid commensurate with their ability, so familiarize yourself with the area where you will have your salon and get a sense of the income of the potential clientele.

You will have to use common sense and a lot of intuition to start out. Your prices will rise, as with all businesses, but you will have to encourage new patrons, give good services, keep your prices within reason, and realize profits to continue. It will take a clever balance of good salesmanship and goodwill to keep you afloat.

Most of your operators will be bringing patrons along with them from their last place of employment, so the practice of paying the operator a percentage will be a workable arrangement for both of you. The percentage must be large enough to induce the operator to continue to work for you and also to want to build up her or his following. Tips are a sizable income source, and most operators realize as much as another thirty to thirty-five percent of their salary in tips.

Hiring an Accountant

Bookkeeping is another very important part of your beauty salon. It is vital to the life of your investment to have accurate bookkeeping. You may have a talent for this area, and in a very small place, you could keep track of all expenditures, income, inventory, repairs, and fees. As your business grows, it is the profit and loss statistics that will guide you in hiring a qualified accountant. Accountants do the job most efficiently and save you money in the long run. A good accountant points out all the areas where you can improve your income, increase your insurance if necessary, cut back on excess personnel, and generally make things orderly. An accountant will be an invaluable aid to you not only in advising you before you purchase a salon, but also in annual bookkeeping. He or she will be able to tell you how to control your expenses and how to realize greater profits. You will also have to deal with business taxes. Your accountant will seem like an expense until you see how difficult it is to figure all the expenditures on your own. Many hours must be spent with the financial juggling of even the smallest business. Tax laws change annually, and the accountant can keep you abreast of all the critical matters without endless hours of research on your part.

Taking Out Insurance

Insurance is another expenditure involved in owning your own place of business. Especially in the cosmetology field, malpractice insurance is a must. Even the most careful operator is human and capable of injuring a customer. A permanent solution could be left on too long, or even after testing, a patron could have a violent allergic reaction. If a patron sues for negligence and wins, you as the salon owner could lose everything that you have worked so hard to build up. Malpractice insurance can protect you, and it is foolhardy not to have it.

Fire insurance is also essential. If the amount of your total investment in your equipment alone were lost, could you afford to replace it? Fire insurance would cover the interior and the exterior of your shop. This kind of insurance should be brought up to date annually, as inflation causes the replacement prices to be higher than the original investment.

Insurance should also cover possible burglary. A few years ago, it would have been extremely uncommon to have equipment stolen from a place like a beauty salon. Now it is wise to cover all equipment, retail stock, and beauty supplies with this type of insurance. The cost of replacing them could mean the difference between closing your business or buying new equipment and starting again.

Liability insurance on the actual premises is another type of insurance that you will have to maintain. If a patron or an employee is injured in your salon, a serious lawsuit could ensue. Depending on the outcome of the damages awarded, a suit could not only put you out of business but into personal debt as well. Accidents can and do happen, and you should be prepared by taking out this kind of insurance.

Some states require that you carry worker's compensation insurance. On-the-job injuries or work-related illness could cause the employee to miss work and lose pay. Worker's compensation pays the employee until he or she can return to work. If your state requires this type of insurance and you are negligent in carrying it, a lawsuit could conceivably put you out of business. Check your state's rulings. Even if your state does not require it, you may find yourself being sued for such a case. Worker's compensation insurance could save you financially.

THE KEY TO SUCCESS

Being nice to your customers is only common sense if you want their business. And happy patrons tell their friends how happy they are with your services. But there is something more than just exterior politeness. You must be honest, fair, loyal, and respectful, not only to the paying clientele but to all your employees as well. Businesslike and considerate methods should keep your salon working at its optimum. If the atmosphere is pleasant and congenial, everyone who comes in touch with your salon will be comfortable and want to return. Your business needs this sort of professionalism to be a lasting success.

CHAPTER 12

BEAUTY SCHOOL OWNERSHIP

Beauty schools can be privately owned or part of a franchise operation where many schools are in the possession of a large business. The statistics are that one in three cosmetologists owns his or her own salon. This statistic has come down from half of all operators in this area having ownership. Barbers have the distinction of 80 percent being owners of their businesses. A portion of these figures then are proprietors of beauty schools and barbering academies.

These schools can be very successful; with all the new laws there are nail schools, aestheticians' schools, and electrologists' schools teaching their fields exclusively.

Graduates in these areas number in the tens of thousands annually. With tuition costs ranging from $2,400 for a license in manicuring to $7,000 for one in hairstyling, you can see that these are solid businesses.

SCHOOLS OF COSMETOLOGY REGULATIONS

Specific regulations spell out every detail set down in state codes. The following regulations are from The Barbering and Cosmetology Act issued by the California Board of Barbering and Cosmetology, New Regulations, 1995.

Approval of Schools

941. (a) To obtain board approval, a private postsecondary school shall submit to the board a request for approval that shall consist of the following:

(1) A document, signed by the owner or owners of the school and certified under penalty of perjury, stating that the school will provide a course of instruction approved by the board and, for cosmetology schools, that all requirements of section 7362.1 of the Business and Professions Code relative to school approval have been met.

(2) A copy of the valid, current Institutional Approval Certificate issued to the school by the Council for Private Postsecondary and Vocational Education.

(b) Within ten working days after receipt of the request for approval as specified in subdivision (a), the board shall notify the school in writing that either the approval is granted or that the request for approval is deficient and what information is required to make the request for approval complete.

(c) The provisions of subdivision (a) must be met for all new schools and schools that have changed ownership or location.

(d) If an approved school no longer meets the requirements of sections 7263 and 7362.1 of the Business and Professions Code, it must notify the board in writing within seven calendar days of what provisions it does not meet.

Cleanliness and Repair

994. (a) Establishments and schools shall keep the floors, walls, woodwork, ceilings, furniture, furnishing, and fixtures clean and in good repair.

(b) No establishment or school shall permit an accumulation of waste or refuse.

Building Standards

995. (a) Establishments and schools shall have a system of adequate ventilation in accordance with the provisions of Section 705 of the Uniform Building Code of 1982, as referenced in Part 2, Chapter 7 of the matrix adoption tables, Title 24, California Code of Regulations.

(b) A supply of hot and cold running water shall be provided in accordance with Part 5, Section 1001(d) (1), Title 24 of the California Code of Regulations.

(c) Establishments and schools shall supply potable drinking water in accordance with Part 5, Section 1001(d) (3), Title 24, California Code of Regulations.

(d) Establishments and schools shall provide hand washing facilities in accordance with Part 5, Section 1001(d) (2), Title 24, California Code of Regulations.

(e) Establishments and schools shall provide public toilet rooms in accordance with Part 5, Sections 910(b), 910(c), and Table No. C–1, Title 24, California Code of Regulations.

Equipment for Schools of Cosmetology

940. (a) The minimum equipment for a school of cosmetology shall be as follows:

1. Sufficient electrical equipment and dermal lights for giving instruction in skin care and electrical facials. Equipment shall be capable of producing galvanic, faradic, and sinusoidal currents. Said electrical equipment and lights shall be required effective October 1, 1980.

2. Ten mannequins, with full head of hair

3. One time clock

4. Five shampoo bowls
   (When the average daily attendance exceeds fifty students, additional shampoo bowls shall be added at the ratio of one for each twenty-five students in average daily attendance in excess of fifty.)

5. Twelve dryers
   (When the average daily attendance exceeds fifty students, additional dryers shall be added at the ratio of one for each ten students in average daily attendance in excess of fifty.)

6. Four facial chairs or facial couches
   (When the average daily attendance exceeds fifty students, additional facial chairs or facial couches shall be added at the ratio of one for each twenty-five students in average daily attendance in excess of fifty.)

7. Six manicure stations
   (When the average daily attendance exceeds fifty students, additional manicure tables shall be added at the ratio of one for each ten students in average daily attendance in excess of fifty.)

8. One electric cap
   (When the average daily attendance exceeds fifty students, additional electrical caps shall be added at the ratio of one for each twenty-five students in average daily attendance in excess of fifty.)

9. Thermal hair straighteners, including:
   three electric combs
   one nonelectric comb
   one electric curling iron
   three nonelectric curling irons (at least two sizes)
   one stove for nonelectric curling irons

(b) The minimum equipment for a school of cosmetology conducting a course in electrology shall also include the following:

1. Either one high frequency generator (thermolysis) machine plus one galvanic generator (electrolysis) machine or one combination thermolysis/electrolysis machine capable of furnishing training in both thermolysis and electrolysis

2. Four needles of various sizes ranging from 0.003 to 0.008 of an inch

3. One dispersive or inactive electrode with connection to the machine, such as wet pad, metal rod, or water jar, necessary for electrology treatments only

4. One lamp and bulb (if bulb is of the exposed type, at least 60-watt strength is required)

5. One stool, adjustable in height

6. One table or chair for patrons

7. One utility stand for set-up

8. One towel cabinet

9. Six covered containers for lotions, soaps, sterilizing agents, and cotton

10. One container for immersing needles for sterilization purposes

11. One container for immersing eye pads in solution

12. One fine-pointed epilation forceps

    (When the average daily attendance of the course of electrology or thermology exceeds three students for a two-month period, one additional complete set of equipment shall be added for each three students in average daily attendance in excess of three.)

(c) The minimum equipment for a school of cosmetology conducting a course in wig styling shall also include the following:

Five blocks in various sizes from nineteen to twenty-three inches with holders.

(When the average daily attendance for students enrolled in a wig styling course exceeds five, additional blocks with holders shall be added at the ratio of one for each additional student.)

(d) Each school shall designate a specific area in which practical training in facials shall be conducted. Such area shall be of sufficient size to accommodate the four facial chairs or couches required by subdivision (a) of this section, and all of such chairs and couches shall remain in the area designated as the facial area at all times during which the school is conducting instruction and training. No chair shall be used as a facial chair unless it is equipped with a headrest and footrest which makes it suitable for the purpose.

Equipment for Schools Conducting a Course in Electrology

912.1. The minimum equipment for a school of electrology and schools of cosmetology conducting a course in electrology shall consist of:

(a) Current Generators:

Either one high frequency generator (thermolysis) and one galvanic generator (electrolysis) machine, or one high frequency generator (thermolysis) and one blend machine capable of producing both the high frequency and galvanic current.

(One additional current generator of those listed above shall be required when the average daily attendance exceeds each multiple of three students.)

(b) The equipment to be used with each required generator shall include:

1. One dozen needles including all graduations from 0.002 to 0.006
2. Lamp and bulb
3. Stool adjustable in height
4. Table or chair for patron
5. Utility stand
6. Sufficient number of covered containers for lotions, soaps, sterilizing agents, contaminated instruments, and cotton
7. Two fine-pointed epilation forceps

(c) Equipment for sterilizing electrolysis needles and tweezers by all the methods prescribed in Section 981

(d) A time clock

Text and Reference Books for Students

961. (a) In teaching, schools shall use text and reference books approved by the board. They may use other teaching material to supplement the approved text and reference books.

(b) Each student shall possess the following:

(1) At least one (1) of the textbooks approved by the board.

(2) The Performance Criteria developed by the board.

(3) The Barbering and Cosmetology Act and the Rules and Regulations of the Board of Barbering and Cosmetology.

(c) There shall be available for the use of students in the school:

(1) A list of the text and reference books approved by the board.

(2) Any two approved texts other than the one text possessed by the student. (Shall not apply to barber schools if there are less than three approved texts.)

The size of the building required by the state will obviously be your first consideration when buying space for a cosmetology school. The state dictates what dimensions are a must. In large cities rental costs could be very expensive. The equipment is also stipulated, and certain numbers of employees will be set by those same boards. All possible financial cost should be weighed carefully, and you should consult with advisors on the best way to start your own business. Rental, buying, or even taking over someone else's established beauty school can all be serious decisions. Mortgages and down payments may be something that you are already familiar with, but if this is your first business, you will want all of the latest advice for taxes and deductions and insurance.

REGULATIONS IN CALIFORNIA

Not all states are as specific as California when it comes to details of cosmetology laws. California's definitions are more precise than many other states' definitions, and for that reason, this state provides a good example.

Course Provider Responsibilities

944. (a) Approved providers shall issue a document of proof, e.g., gradeslip or transcript, to each licensee to show that he or she has met the established criteria for successful completion of a course. The certificates of proof documenting successful completion shall contain the following information:

(1) Name of student and license number.

(2) Course title.

(3) Provider name (as approved by the board), address, and provider number.

(4) Date of course.

(5) Number of continuing education hours completed.

(6) Signature of instructor and/or provider, or provider designee.

(b) Course verification shall be issued by the provider within ninety (90) days after the completion of the course, not to exceed ninety days.

(c) Approved providers shall maintain course verification certificates for at least four years from the date the course was completed.

(d) Approved providers shall have a written and published policy, available on request, which provides information on:

(1) Refunds in cases of non-attendance.

(2) Time period for return of fees.

(3) Notification if course is canceled.

(e) Approved providers may not grant partial credit for continuing education courses.

(f) Approved providers shall notify the board within thirty (30) days of any changes in organizational structure of a provider and a change in the person(s) responsible for the provider's continuing education course(s).

(g) (1) Within seven (7) calendar days of receipt of an application for approval as an approved provider, the board shall inform the applicant in writing that the application is either complete and accepted for filing or that it is deficient and what specific information or documentation is required to complete the application.

(2) Within seven (7) calendar days from the date of filing of a completed application for approval as an approved provider, the board shall inform the applicant in writing of its decision regarding an application.

(h) (1) Within ten (10) calendar days of receipt of an application for approval of a continuing education course, the board shall inform the applicant in writing that the application is either complete and accepted for filing or that it is deficient and what specific information or documentation is required to complete the application.

(2) Within forty-two (42) calendar days from the date of filing of a completed application for approval of a continuing education course, the board shall inform the applicant in writing of its decision regarding an application.

Course Approval

945. (a) An approved provider shall submit to the board all material deemed necessary to judge the quality of the program on the basis of the factors stated in subdivision (b). The board shall grant or deny approval on the basis of educational quality and compliance with all requirements of law and regulation.

(b) For a course to be granted approval, it must:

(1) Be sponsored by an approved provider.

(2) Include a certificate of completion.

(3) Include some mechanism (test, self-administered or otherwise) whereby participants can evaluate comprehension of material.

(4) Include stated goals and specific instructional objectives.

(5) Include a complete and sound syllabus.

(6) Consist of material which is accurate, orderly, complete, and applicable to the teaching of vocational education.

Approved Providers

943. (a) The following continuing education providers have been approved by the board to provide continuing education:

(1) Any local education agency, currently approved by the California Commission on Teacher Credentialing, which offers a program of personalized preparation for a vocational education teaching credential.

(2) Public and private postsecondary schools accredited by the Western Association of Schools and Colleges.

(b) A person or organization may request approval to act as a continuing education provider by submitting the request in writing to the board.

(c) An approved continuing education provider may request course approval from the board by submitting a course approval request which includes course description of the proposed course. The content of the course or program shall be designed for continuing education in the teaching of vocational education and may include, but not be limited to, development of understanding and competency in the learning process, instructional techniques, curriculum and media, instructional evaluation, counseling and guidance, and the special needs of students. All continuing education course work shall be based upon stated educational objectives. Continuing education course work shall not be designed to promote the commercial products of the provider or of any persons giving financial assistance to the provider.

Provider Advertising

946. Information disseminated by a recognized provider publicizing continuing education shall be true and not misleading and shall include the following:

(a) The statement "Provider recognized by the Calif. Board of Barbering and Cosmetology, Provider Number _____ for _____ hours."

(b) Provider's policy on refunds in cases of non-attendance by the registrant.

(c) A clear, concise description of the course content and/or objectives.

(d) Provider name as officially on file with the board.

Provider Instructor Qualifications

948. Instructors teaching approved continuing education courses shall either hold a baccalaureate or higher degree from an accredited college or university and validated experience in the subject matter; or holds a credential to teach vocational education full time in a public school in this state.

Authority to Audit Records and Rescind Provider Status

949. (a) The board retains the right and authority to audit records or monitor courses given by any recognized provider.

(b) The board shall audit licensee records regarding continuing education hours completed as it deems necessary to assure that the continuing education requirements are met.

(c) The board may rescind recognized provider status if the provider has disseminated any false or misleading information in connection with the continuing education program, or if the provider has failed to conform to the provisions of this Article.

Requirements for (Continuing Education) Instructors

942. (a) All instructors shall retain for at least four years:

(1) Certificates of completion of the continuing education courses obtained through a recognized provider.

(2) Information regarding the completion of continuing education courses obtained through an approved provider, including name of provider, course title and number, date completed, and number of units or hours.

(b) Any licensee who knowingly furnishes false or misleading information to the board regarding continuing education hours shall be subject to disciplinary action.

(c) Of the 30 hours of approved continuing education in the teaching of vocational education required during each two-year licensing period, a maximum of 15 hours may be in teaching methods relative to barbering and cosmetology practical operations.

Continuing Education Hours

947. (a) Each hour of theory shall be accepted as one clock hour of continuing education.

(b) One academic quarter unit is equal to 10 clock hours of continuing education.

(c) One academic semester unit is equal to 15 clock hours of continuing education.

Schedule of Fees

998.   Barber Instructors:

Application, examination and initial license fee	50
License renewal fee	40[1]
License renewal delinquency fee	20[1]

Cosmetology Instructors:

Application, examination and initial license fee	50
License renewal fee	40[1]
License renewal delinquency fee	20[1]
Apprentice application and license fee	25

Establishments:

Application and initial license fee	50
License renewal fee	40[1]
License renewal delinquency fee	20[1]

---

[1]Fees effective for all licenses expiring on or after July 31, 1993.

All states have similar stipulations for owning a school of cosmetology, though they do not have as many restrictions, and they are usually not as well defined as these. The operation of a school of this nature takes serious endeavor on the part of the owner or owners. The success of the school depends on the owner's ability to meet all the financial needs, the legal prerequisites, and the needs of the staff and students. Location and student enrollment obviously dictate income potential.

There are strict health regulations that govern the physical plant as to plumbing, floor coverings, windows (number of and coverings for), fire code compliance, number and sanitation of toilets, and provisions for pest control. Cleanliness and sanitation are paramount in a beauty school due to the nature of its services.

CHAPTER 13

SALON MANAGERS AND MANAGER–OPERATORS

Recent laws in several states now regulate managers of beauty salons who are cosmetologists, manicurists, and aestheticians. In most states as long as you hold a valid license in cosmetology and have been employed in that profession for a specified number of years, your qualifications are met. The detailed managerial licenses are in the following states: Delaware, Maryland, Minnesota, North Dakota, Ohio, and South Dakota. Be sure to research the specific laws of the state where you will be employed as a manager. They are not widely different in actual time and experience requirement, but the legal terminology does vary. Minnesota and Ohio alone require specific licenses to be held by manicurist managers. Ohio is the only state to offer a license for the aesthetician manager.

The position of the managing cosmetologist (manager–operator) is often considered the intermediate post between doing cosmetological work and owning a salon. Each state dictates prerequisites, such as the amount of schooling needed, years of cosmetology experience, and manager–operator licensing. A manager–cosmetologist earns an annual income of about $25,000 in larger cities. The actual number of patrons whom a cosmetologist brings to the salon for weekly services has a great effect on his or her salary level.

Certain managerial positions are geared toward promotion, while others are strictly business coordination. The emphasis depends on the size of the salon and the salary arrangement.

One New York City department store manager considers his main responsibility as business. He does not dress hair, nor does he have to be

93

licensed by the state of New York. He is a man of responsibility, charm, and efficiency. His work consists of hiring, firing, maintaining inventory, overseeing the bookkeeping, and seeing to schedules for daily work and holidays for all employees. He is paid a percentage of the salon's profits and feels that this arrangement gives him more incentive to work, as his income is not limited.

The manager–operator must be licensed as a cosmetologist by the state in which he or she works. The manager–operator is permitted to touch the patron and do hairstyles, unlike the manager who is not a cosmetologist. States require varying levels of experience as a licensed operator before application can be made for the manager–operator license. Some states will permit operators to apply for that particular license as soon as they have started to work in a salon.

The advantage of having been an operator prior to taking a managerial position is that being familiar with all aspects of the cosmetology business is helpful in numerous ways. You may be permitted to suggest improvements, such as the introduction of new equipment or even a cosmetic line bearing your salon's signature. All of these factors directly influence your income.

A MANAGER'S RESPONSIBILITIES

As a manager–cosmetologist, you would be directly responsible for the entire coordination and running of the business. Linens have to be rented and laundered, supplies have to be kept in stock, and equipment has to be kept up-to-date and in working order.

It would be your obligation to keep abreast of regulations, and you would have to read new codes annually. The decor of the salon may be one of your responsibilities. You must learn to balance economy with attractive surroundings. There are many kinds of managerial positions, so you will definitely want to have all of your areas of authority spelled out clearly.

Avoid being in a position where more and more work is expected of you without salary adjustments. You will be managing the largest portion of the business end of the salon. With the exception of paying rent or mortgage payments and directing funds for business expenses, you could conceivably be running the entire salon. You may even be managing the money for the owners. Coordinating the entire operation and suffering the headaches that accompany that amount of responsibility makes the manager's position the highest paid of the salon employees.

The wage scale varies from state to state, salon to salon. Anything above minimum wage, and often well above $450 a week can be expected in larger cities. The location of the salon will definitely have an influence on your salary. If the customers are paying above average for services, the salary for a manager would be comparable. In a small local salon, the responsibilities may be of greater variety, but the pay would obviously have to be in line with the income of the shop.

Managers are normally expected to work the longest hours as well. A manager has to oversee the entire workings of the salon and must be aware of problems before they become too difficult to handle.

The hiring of personnel is very important. Keeping a happy, congenial group must always be paramount in the manager's mind. One unpleasant employee, no matter how talented, can cause miserable working conditions for everyone in the salon.

The quality of the workmanship is what will make or break your salon's future. If you do have skilled hairstylists, word-of-mouth will interest others, and your clientele will increase.

One of the jobs of the manager is unfortunately policing. He or she has to make certain that all licenses are current for every operator, the salon, and of course for him or herself if the state requires a manager's license.

Enforcement of all sanitary rules is also one of a manager's responsibilities. If your salon suffered a lawsuit because one of your operators was negligent, your employer, the salon owner, would certainly be looking for a new manager. So to protect yourself and everyone else, policy should be clearly stated at the beginning, and everyone will know what is expected of him or her and how he or she is to conduct him or herself under your management. In case of a critical problem, management will have to be the arbitrator, and short of a lawsuit, your wisdom will have to prevail. Experience is usually a great help when these crises arise, but there will always be a "first," and how you handle the situation will be noted by your underlings as well as your boss.

Diplomat, overseer, personnel coordinator, inventory controller, host, record and schedule keeper—these are the responsibilities of the manager.

The number of positions open to managers are few. Many salon owners prefer to manage their own salons. If you are interested in management, you may do well to consult trade periodicals and a large city newspaper's want ads.

CHAPTER 14

COMPETITION HAIRSTYLISTS

The person who starts entering hairstyle competitions soon learns how to prepare a model's hair with strict specifications for a particular look. All the details are spelled out and the contest is then judged by experienced cosmetologists in the field. Competitions could be as simple as a daytime hairstyle for the office all the way to a cut, color, and evening style with hair ornaments. It is really fun to attend these competitions just to observe the top potential of those technicians in your chosen field. Not only can you become inspired by their creativity but you can learn many tricks of the trade by watching their timesaving moves.

There are many reasons you might want to enter hairdressers' competitions. If you are planning on making a career in hairstyling, you really should consider applying to as many competitions as possible. There are numerous benefits. You will meet many people in your chosen field, and you will be able to observe firsthand the best cosmetologists. Exposure to many clever hairdressers is a tremendous learning experience.

You have the advantage of being able to enter competitions as early as your days in beauty school. The confidence that you can gain in competition is worth every penny of your entrance fees. Competitions are also very exciting. Prizes range from trophies to cash, and many contacts are made during these shows that can lead to recognition in the cosmetology world. The press covers all the proceedings, and many fine cosmetologists have gained a following through competition.

COMPETITIONS

Hair competition for a cosmetology student would most likely consist of a daytime haircut, style, or other already familiar technique. The experience of competing gives the student a better idea of accuracy, speed, and the correct method of attaining an end result at someone's request. When the pressure is on, some students function at their best. Others simply cannot cope with all the confusion and noise and are better off in the slower pace of school. This does not mean that if you have trouble at your first competition you should not consider entering competitions in the future, after you have gained experience and confidence.

There are also competitions for students of barbering schools who must quickly and skillfully perform a man's cut and present their model with a final polished look. The haircut itself may be judged separately.

Competitions are sponsored by a variety of groups. The most common sponsor is the larger manufacturer of products like hairdressings or makeup, publishers of cosmetology magazines, and affiliations of cosmetologists. Competitions occur frequently.

Areas of Competition

The professional has many different choices of areas in which to compete. One specialty for competition is permanent waving. There are many ways in which hair can be set and styled to achieve a particular look. The choice of wrapping method makes a remarkable difference. The corkscrew method of curling the hair on the rod is a recent technique. You could perm only the base of the hair, or only the ends of the hair, or the entire length of the hair. All of these techniques give a wide variety of hairstyles and enable you to achieve innovative results.

Time allotment is critical, so have everything organized in your mind ahead of time. Judges are usually a panel of several authorities in the field. You will be told the theme or silhouette to be achieved, and whether it is to be a daytime or evening hairstyle. Be certain that you and your model are available at the prescribed hour, as latecomers are turned away, and your entrance fee probably will not be refunded.

Some possible competitions could be creative coloring, creative or "open" hairstyling (the contestant can create any style or type of hair design such as high fashion, day, or evening), men's styling competition by a cosmetologist (no barbers permitted to enter), creative cutting, or dual competition, wherein one male and one female model are styled by the same contestant to show the operator's ability to "cross over." (Formerly, *unisex* was the term used to describe hairstyling for both men and women.) There are competitions for permanent waving, and even contests wherein the cosmetologist creates an entire fashion look. The contestant coordinates hair, makeup, and even clothing to present a total look.

REASONS FOR COMPETING

Competitions are held at the lower levels for the operator to gain experience, to develop a better time record for setting and comb-outs, and to acquire a reputation. Winning competitions is a good way to become recognized and to increase clientele. Sometimes the prize is money, a trophy, or a plaque engraved with recognition of award or merit. Many operators and beauty salon owners announce their most prestigious awards in their advertisements and on business cards.

One of the best reasons to enter competition is just for fun. It is an opportunity for creativity and innovation. When you work in a salon, you must consider the wishes of the client. Not so at competitions! Restrictions are set down prior to entering, and you can enter the competition of your choice as long as you are qualified. You supply your own model and work with him or her exclusively. The rules will dictate to the letter what colors are acceptable and how they may be used, what type of rollers or clips you may use and even how you are to dry hair. Any electric devices you will need have to be stated prior to the onset of the competition, and you will be advised as to available outlets and wattage.

Competitions are a chance for you to learn by observing. The best in the field are represented at competitions, and you can watch genuine talent. By the time that the advanced and very highly skilled cosmetologists are competing, the prizes are more prestigious. International teams enter against other famous international teams in Olympic hairstyling competitions. As you might have guessed, these contests are quite spectacular for hair fashion as well as for the latest in clothing. Designer clothes and hairstyles blend in this level of competition, and the model is presented with a complete look. Even if a model is dressed in the most glamorous gown, the effect is ruined if her hair is not styled properly. So this is where the hairstylist can really shine. A beautiful and well-thought-out hair creation (one that truly benefits the model and the mood) can make the whole presentation.

Hair competition can keep you well abreast of current styles. For a competition, no dated hairstyle is requested or permitted. There are many benefits to be gained from entering contests: education, experience, a wider scope of the field of cosmetology (particularly how it fits into the beauty world), confidence in yourself and in your chosen craft, recognition for personal ability and talents as well as publicity and status for the salon that you own or where you are currently employed, and last, but not least, your awards in trophy or cash prizes.

There are endless competitions at all levels of experience and talent. You may want to compete alone or as a team member from your salon. You may some day be talented and famous enough to compete on the international level with years of solid experience behind you and recognition throughout the entire cosmetology world. The best part of entering competition styling is that it is wide open to students, professionals, small-town salon operators and big-city, high fashion stylists, males, and females. You will never know what you could be winning unless you compete!

CHAPTER 15

THE PLATFORM HAIRSTYLIST

Many hair product manufacturers hire the platform hairstylist to demonstrate their wares to beauty schools, beauty salons, and the public via hair shows. These very talented artists work with hair and all its sundry associated accoutrements such as dyes, cuts, styles, and the newest trends. These specialists demand very high salaries and are often paid per hour wages of $75 to $150. The creative ability of the platform artist sets him or her apart from other cosmetologists by the highly polished technical work that is accomplished quickly and with near perfect results. This stylist thus becomes a liaison between the world of the newest created fashion and the world of the cosmetologists who must recreate this look for the public, their clients. The most popularized looks on the fashion runway or in the live concerts or movies are brought to the salons. One of the latest hairstyles in great demand is what is referred to as *Natural Hair Styling*. It has become so popular that a license is required in several states to perform its arranging, twisting, weaving, wrapping, and braiding. Licensing became a necessity due to some untrained technicians putting too much tension on the hair roots during the aforementioned processes, with damage resulting to the scalp and hair of patrons.

In New York state, you may qualify for your license in Natural Hair Styling just by having a year of past experience, or you could attend a beauty school to obtain this specialty license. This could be one of the hair techniques taught by the platform stylist as it is very trendy and many clients might ask for this look.

THE ROLE OF THE PLATFORM STYLIST

Platform stylists are really teachers with much more savvy and aware-ness of hair trends—both immediate and future—than the average opera-tor. Most teachers and operators are engrossed in the daily routine of styling patrons' hair. Keeping up-to-date is a critical problem for all hair-stylists. Unless a style is acceptably current, few patrons will want to wear it. Even the standby short permed hairstyle for the elderly patron has become softer and more natural looking. So not only must operators know present hairstyles, but a good operator must have a constant aware-ness of the latest trend and even future trends. Younger people in particu-lar are extremely demanding in their desire to wear the latest trend or even be pacesetters. There are many salons whose managers hire plat-form stylists regularly to enlighten the entire staff.

It would be extremely costly and, in a small salon, truly impossible for all the cosmetologists to return to school as often as hair fashions change. With a platform stylist visiting and teaching in the beauty sa-lon, every person benefits. The operators do not have to lose even a day's work since the platform stylist is usually scheduled to give lec-tures and demonstrations during the hours immediately before or di-rectly after the salon's business hours. By being in the work environment, the operator can more easily visualize how and with what equipment new hairstyles will be created. Busier salons can afford to have a few operators ask the platform stylist questions during lengthier sessions as other operators continue to work. Some instructors do plat-form stylist work as well as beauty school instruction on an advanced level. There are many ways in the beauty industry to combine the vari-ous aspects of the cosmetology trade, just as long as you are practicing in a state that does not require more education than you have or a dif-ferent license from the one that you hold.

The platform stylist teaches only techniques, and continuing educa-tion courses are geared to business and management.

BECOMING A PLATFORM STYLIST

The platform stylist can expect to earn about $400 for four to eight hours of work. Some very famous platform stylists earn $1,000 a day for their instruction. Supply houses, cosmetic firms, and sometimes affiliates sponsor platform stylists. A normal schedule for a well-qualified platform stylist might be giving lectures and instruction only twice a month. It is not an everyday job, and most of these "teachers" work in managerial or operator positions in salons. Some platform stylists take their lecture, instruction, slides, and models from place to place. But their schedule is almost never full time.

The platform stylist's work necessitates both having up-to-the-second information on the "in" hairstyle and knowing how to create it. The former is obviously easier to come by. Some of the complexities of accomplishing a particular look are really very trying. It takes patience and an adaptable mind to be able to master one technique after another. Some extremely complex styles demand hours of fine hair coloring and then several more hours of hair wrapping to achieve the desired outcome. Often, shortly after gaining proficiency in a certain technique, that technique is on its way out. Then you have to struggle to grasp the new technique before you lose customers who desire the new hairstyle.

Hairdressing is very much a part of the fashion world and change is constant. It is a challenge to some operators, and an impossibility for others, to learn the new techniques necessary to create the latest trend. Somehow it has always been the innovators in the hairdressing world, like those in the fashion world of clothing, who have caught the attention of the fashion-conscious and held it over the years. Very avant-garde hairstyles, such as the asymmetricals a few years ago, are just what the fashion people love. Hairstylists spark their imaginations and give them a creating force or impetus. Hairstylists must have constant input; the fashion world never stands still. The platform stylist is therefore very necessary. And with a reasonable amount of ambition and perseverance it can be a very rewarding job.

Another advantage of working as a platform stylist is the potential for travel. But extensive travel may not be necessary. If you want to stay in a general vicinity, taking your newly learned knowledge to an area with a smaller radius, you could conceivably stay within several counties or states. Or you could find yourself lecturing in other countries. As fashion travels, so must hairstyle techniques. We in the United States often adapt French or English hair fashions. This offers a great opportunity for the platform stylist to learn the method and transport it.

FINDING A JOB

A platform stylist often finds work through first establishing himself or herself as a competition stylist. The demand for his or her work could eventually lead to actual platform work when available.

In certain states, a platform license is required. This license is applied for only once and lasts as long as the stylist maintains an active cosmetology license.

Work as a platform stylist can be acquired through hiring a booking agent. Some stylists simply freelance if their contacts are already established through a hairdressing affiliate

CHAPTER 16

FUTURE JOB OUTLOOK
FOR COSMETOLOGISTS

JOB OPPORTUNITIES

The United States Department of Labor's 1994 edition of the *Occupational Outlook Handbook* offers the following projections for opportunities in cosmetology.

There will be 239,000 new jobs by 2005 for those in the cosmetology industry, approximately 18,384 new openings per year. An estimated 218,000 of the new positions will be filled by hairdressers alone. The total numbers of barbers and cosmetologists combined are 746,000. Of these numbers 671,400 are cosmetologists. The job outlook is noted as being faster than the average for other employment right through the year 2005. Cosmetologists and manicurists account for the major increases as the barbers decline slightly. Many barbers have discovered that they must do hairstyling to stay competitive.

The projection for earnings in this field is between $25,000 and $35,000 a year depending on the area of the United States. The number of clientele and the amount of your tips have a direct impact on your earnings. The entire revenue paid to cosmetologists in 1992 was $11,999 million, of which $3,530 million was payroll to 390,700 employees. The annual payroll per employee was $9,055. (Tips made up the rest.)

The projected increase then will continue at the rate of approximately three to seven thousand per annum depending on the aforementioned factors of geographic location, number of customers and of course the cost of the cosmetological procedures.

In 1994, there were about 671,400 cosmetologists employed in the United States. They worked in beauty shops, unisex shops, department stores, hospitals, and hotels. In 1986, statistics show that 595,000 persons were employed cosmetologists. At that time, the projected growth was excellent. It is obvious that this particular field is expanding greatly, and if it continues at the indicated pace, there will be many jobs available through the 2000s.

In California alone, there are approximately 50,000 employed cosmetologists, and the projected job openings in that state are 4,550 per year. Nearly 10,000 cosmetology students graduate every year from California beauty schools. Though this situation has existed for several years, it does not seem to have affected the demand for cosmetologists in California, according to the *California Occupational Guide.*

Even if the projections are somewhat contradictory, the overall picture for the future of cosmetology is an exceptionally bright one. There are many people who complete cosmetology schooling, take the state boards, become licensed operators, and then do not seek full-time employment. The statistics only tell us how many persons hold cosmetology licenses and do not go into detail as to how often, or even if, many of these operators join in the work force. There will always be openings for qualified hairstylists. The demand is continuing and growing. All the cosmetology services need to be filled to capacity, and there are jobs continuously becoming available.

SALARIES

Average earnings for a cosmetologist who is just starting out amount to between $12,500 and $15,600 per year. The projected increase is about $25,000 as soon as he or she has an established clientele. Remember that this is an average figure, and that there are cities where the salary could be much higher and less-populated areas where it could be lower. Tips are notably larger in the bigger cities and easily could amount to one-third of the wage.

Salaries and commissions normally are negotiated before an operator accepts a position with a salon. Much depends upon the experience and the following that the operator is bringing into the salon. If a large following will accompany the operator, it is not in his or her best interest to settle for a straight salary. Obviously the clientele will continue to increase, and the operator should benefit as well as the salon owner.

Commission arrangements are normally forty to fifty percent of the total for the operator. Only if an operator had no following and was just starting out would he or she consider a minimum guaranteed salary. Specialists and stylists with experience earned salaries around $20,000 a year in the mid- and late 1980s. Those same operators are probably earning more than $25,000 today plus tips.

The salon owner who was earning approximately $10,000 in 1979 is probably earning $32,000 today. Inflation has caused the price of all service to rapidly increase, and the products that the salon uses are not increasing in the same proportion. Larger salons were experiencing even more rapid growth during the past three years. More prestigious salons can afford to pay their operators a smaller salary in many cases because the operator wants to benefit by working next to recognized and highly skilled hairstylists. So, you can see that salaries do not always meet with expectations. Ultimately, you will have to choose between accepting a higher salary now, and perhaps having it remain the same for several years, or taking the lesser salary now, with an eye to the future when you have acquired a fine technique.

The franchise owner's average salary was projected to be somewhere between $22,000 and $29,000 a year in the 1990s. You can see that the franchise owner's income is similar to the skilled stylist's annual salary.

WORKING CONDITIONS

There may or may not be added benefits for an operator who is employed by a salon. Sometimes group health and life insurance policies cover the operator, and vacations may or may not be included. Paid vacations are now quite common.

The long hours and the pressures of the job should be taken into consideration. Most of your work will be on the weekends when your patrons want to look their best. Some salons even have Sunday hours. So find out the schedules of the salon where you are contemplating employment and weigh all of the pros and cons carefully. Cosmetology can bring you many hours of pleasure and a wonderfully secure future. The ideal is simply to work at the location and for the number of hours that will make you the happiest.

CHAPTER 17

STATE BOARDS OF COSMETOLOGY

The legal arm of cosmetology sets the standards for what can be performed in the field with the public good as first consideration. The newest legislation passed by some of these boards addresses more stringent health codes and environmental concerns. For example, the fungus infections prevalent in nail care became so problematic that lawsuits ensued. New laws were then passed to guarantee that all manicurists be licensed in New York state as well as several other states. The awareness that the fungus was being transmitted from client to client brought about stricter laws for sterilization of all metal instruments, particularly those used to trim cuticle matter. The other instruments used in manicuring and pedicuring then needed to be personalized so that each patron had an exclusive set. Some salons chose to supply these individualized kits while others could not afford the added expense and patrons brought their own. The public good thus forced changes to occur shortly after the first lawsuits pointed to the need for more sanitary conditions.

In every state there is a body that makes the rules and regulations for all cosmetologists, their businesses, and their associations. In California it is called the Board of Barbering and Cosmetology, and variations of that title are used in every state. These boards exist to protect you and the public. They can deny your license renewal through revocation or suspension. They can actually enforce disqualification if just cause is shown. So find out about your state's regulations. Be informed.

The state boards were established to protect the consumer, to elevate cosmetology to a higher level, and to maintain that level through the continuation of the board itself. New members of the board are selected by appointment and hold their given posts for varying numbers of years, depending on the state.

The Chapter 477, Florida Statutes Title: Florida Cosmetology Act, states the following:

Purpose

477.012. The legislature recognizes that the practice of cosmetology involves the use of tools and chemicals which may be dangerous when applied improperly and, therefore, deems it necessary in the interest of public health to regulate the practice of cosmetology in this state. However, restrictions shall be imposed only to the extent necessary to protect the public from significant and discernible danger to health and not in a manner which will unreasonably affect the competitive market. Further, consumer protection for both health and economic matters shall be afforded the public through legal remedies provided for in this act.

Board of Cosmetology

477.015. (1) There is created within the department the Board of Cosmetology consisting of seven members, who shall be appointed by the Governor, subject to confirmation by the Senate, and whose function it shall be to carry out the provisions of this act.

(2) Five members of the board shall be licensed cosmetologists and shall have been engaged in the practice of cosmetology in this state for not less than 5 years. Two members of the board shall be lay persons. Each board member shall be a resident of this state and shall have been a resident of this state for not less than 5 continuous years.

(3) The Governor may at any time fill vacancies on the board for the remainder of the unexpired terms. Each member of the board shall hold over after the expiration of his term until a successor is duly appointed and qualified. No board member shall serve more than two consecutive terms, whether full or partial.

(4) Before assuming his duties as a board member, each appointee shall take the constitutional oath of office and shall file it with the Department of State, which shall then issue to such member a certificate of his appointment.

(5) The board shall, in the month of January, elect from its number a chairman and a vice chairman.

(6) The board shall hold such meetings during the year as it may determine to be necessary, one of which shall be the annual meeting. The chairman of the board shall have the authority to call other meetings at his discretion. A quorum of the board shall consist of not less than four members.

(7) Each member of the board shall receive $50 for each day spent in the performance of official board business, with the total annual compensation per member not to exceed $2,000. Additionally, board members shall receive per diem and mileage as provided in s. 112.061, from place of residence to place of meeting and return.

(8) Each board member shall be held accountable to the Governor for the proper performance of all his duties and obligations. The Governor shall investigate any complaints or unfavorable reports received concerning the actions of the board, or its members, and shall take appropriate action thereon, which action may include removal of any board member. The Governor may remove from office any board member for neglect of duty, incompetence, or unprofessional or dishonorable conduct.

In North Carolina, a three-member board is appointed by the governor. The board is known as the State Board of Cosmetic Arts. This board appoints necessary inspectors who are experienced in all areas of cosmetic art. These inspectors make expert reports to the board. Official business of the board includes four annual meetings, supervising and administering examinations, investigations, or inspections. The board also submits a fiscal budget to cover the board's expenses.

In Texas, the Texas Cosmetology Commission consists of six members appointed by the governor. The commission must meet at least once a year. The commission may issue rules, prescribe school curricula for the cosmetology schools, prescribe the content of the examinations, and establish the sanitary rules that pertain to cosmetology.

In New York state, the advisory committee is the equivalent of the cosmetology board in other states. This committee consists of nine members. It is their job to advise the secretary of state on all matters relating to hairdressing and cosmetology.

California has a nine-member board that administers examinations of all applicants for registration, issues certificates of registration, registers cosmetological establishments and cosmetology schools, reports all violations to proper authorities, holds investigations and inquiries, adopts sanitary rules and regulations, and makes an annual report to the governor concerning the condition of cosmetology and its affiliated branches. A financial statement accompanies this report and lists the expenditures and monies received from fees, licenses, registrations, and applications.

It is important to know the duties performed by your state's board and to know what laws protect you. The governing bodies that create the cosmetology tests and rules affect what you can and cannot do. You should read the specific rules and regulations for the state in which you will be practicing. The state board is a political branch of cosmetology, and you may be interested in being part of it one day. Take an interest in who is making the rules, and write to the state board if you feel that something is unfair. As a cosmetologist, the board represents you at the state level, and you have a stake in its decisions.

For a state-by-state listing of Boards of Cosmetology, see Appendix D.

CHAPTER 18

COSMETOLOGY IN CANADA

Having a hairstyling or barbering career in Canada is considered not only a financially secure but also a very exciting venture. Many technicians in the industry are happily employed, from small towns and part time jobs to very busy, big city salons where they work over eight hours a day. The television production crews are often in need of these hairstylist technicians. A great number of the television shows that we see are created in Canada, and many of those numbers are shot in Toronto. Where there is theatre, be it live or filmed, the call for cosmetologists just increases. Viewers want to keep up with the facial looks and hairstyles that are portrayed. The demand for good hairstylists has increased in Canada just as it has in the United States.

In 1994, there were 23,073 beauty salons dispersed across Canada. Most of these shops were grouped in the urban centers. While one might have expected a larger number, there were only 5,489 barbershops spread throughout the provinces. In the five years between 1985 and 1990, the cosmetology industry grew by 10,295 persons, an increase of 2,059 individuals per year. The concentration of these employees was accounted for in the largest cities. During this same time frame, the numbers of full time workers went from 42,795 to 53,390 cosmetological technicians. Interestingly, the number of male operators increased by 10,875. About 2,175 more women joined the ranks annually.

The wages paid to the male technicians alone were $24,151 in 1990, while the female employees during that same period gleaned $16,785. This disparity could be because the women may not have been self-employed, owned as many of the salons wherein they worked, or perhaps were employed in lower income areas. These statistics were cited from the 1991 Census of Canada, Catalogue #93.332.

Canadian hairstylists and barbers are employed in hairdressing salons, barber shops, health care establishments, and theatre, film, and television establishments. (According to the Minister of Supply and Services, Canada 1993 Catalogue #MP53–25/1–1993E.)

Work descriptions for hairstylists and their main duties in Canada are as follows: these operators cut, trim, perm, wave, curl, and style the hair. They guide the client as to the services rendered in determining appropriate cut, shape, color, and style. Coloring and dying the hair, or bleaching, frosting, and/or highlighting are also part of their duties. Treatments for hair and scalp and the analysis of same are encompassed by the hairstylist. Instruction duties may or may not be required of a particular operator, but the supervisory duties are expected when there is a need. Other names or titles are hair colour technician, hairdresser, hairdresser apprentice, hairstylist apprentice, or wig stylist.

Barbers are expected to cut facial hair as well as the hair on the head. They may do shampooing, dying, perms, and treatments for the scalp and hair. A barber must have some secondary school before embarking on the formal training to barber. He or she then goes through a two-year apprenticeship or courses in barbering. A license or certification is required, though these differ from province to province.

Hairstylists need to complete some secondary education prior to starting formal cosmetological studies. An extended apprenticeship of from two to three years could qualify you for your employment requirements or you could acquire your education in a college or cosmetology school. Again, provincial certification and/or licensing are needed to work legally anywhere in Canada. This information comes from the Minister of Supply and Services, Canada 1993 Catalogue #MP53–25/1–1993E.

HAIRSTYLING SCHOOL

Hairstyling programs in Canada are largely located in or near the larger urban areas, so if you find it difficult to locate a beauty school near you, write to one of the Canadian Cosmetology Associations listed on the last page of this chapter. They can be very helpful in suggesting a school suitable to your needs.

The hairstyling school that I will use as an example here requires an applicant to have a minimum education of ninth grade and to be at least sixteen years of age prior to registration. Proof of education needs written documentation that the applicant has had courses including English, science, and mathematics. If it is not possible to have written documentation, the school will administer a Canadian Adult Achievement Test. Both day and evening courses are offered at this particular school. The hours are daily from 8:30 A.M. to 4:30 P.M. for about ten months a year. The evening course is for a duration of approximately 20 months and is given during the hours of 5:00 to 9:30 three evenings a week and for six and a half hours on Saturday. So you can see that a variation on the school schedules can be arranged to fit your current agenda. The tuition costs are $3,500 for either program. This includes the registration fee, tuition, and a package of textbooks, uniform, and hairstyling supplies. This particular school offers barbering techniques in its curriculum as well as the usual hairstyling methods.

AESTHETICIANS, ELECTROLOGISTS, AND TATTOO ARTISTS

These operators are able to find employment in beauty salons, electrologist salons, hair and facial salons, and tattoo parlours. The aesthetician (also spelled esthetician) administers facials manually and with electrical machines. The work is often done in luxurious surroundings and is quite well paid, with the added bonus of usually substantial tipping. The work is done while standing and leaning over a massage table or a reclining facial chair. The major drawback would be extended hours of being on your feet.

Aestheticians are also known as makeup artists. They most often find employment in the world of modeling, television, and theater. It is rare that a beauty salon could have enough clients to keep a makeup artist busy, let alone well paid. Some makeup artists choose to work for cosmetic companies. There they demonstrate the products on clients usually in department stores, boutiques, or in the cosmetic company's training program. The reason you would want to be licensed as an aesthetician is that you could then advance in the field unhampered by restrictive laws. It is important when working with makeup to be able to actually touch the face while applying color, and prohibiting laws in various areas could prevent you from doing this. The other title for an aesthetician who applies makeup is a cosmetician. It is not unusual for makeup artists to establish themselves as independent technicians who work on weddings, have some appointments at a few selected beauty salons, and work on modeling shoots. The way this work is procured is often through apprenticing with an established makeup artist as an assistant. After getting to know all the tricks of the trade, you could start establishing yourself on small jobs and work from there. This could be an exciting and often glamorous career.

Tattoo artists most often work out of their own studios or a shared area with another operator from the cosmetological field. The work can be very creative; the art of tattooing has had a tremendous revival in the past few years. Famous athletes and rock stars sport tattoos as do many actors and actresses. Many famous bodies have several tattoos adorning the anatomy in strategic places. Tattoos are permanently applied to the skin through the use of electrical needles and dyes. There is a method of erasing these tattoos now, but it is not all that comfortable, so a tattoo should be a serious consideration before it is applied to a person's body. To be a tattoo artist, you have to have completed required schooling and then have either formal training or on-the-job training. You need to check with your provincial authorities to ascertain the licensing requirement. Salary for the tattoo artist depends entirely on what kind of following he or she has established. Word of mouth is definitely the best advertisement—as is the visibility of the creative tattoos themselves. They have always been a source of fascination, conjuring up visions of romantic sea voyages or of the islanders of the South Pacific who originally inspired the tattoo.

Electrologists may find employment in beauty salons or in studios of their own. Often the electrologist is self employed but shares his or her space with another technician. The services performed by the electrologist are those of permanent removal of facial or body hair. The hair is removed by electrical needles that destroy the hair follicle. Many customers are extremely happy with this treatment as it is a finite solution to an often embarrassing problem. Since our society dictates just where and how much body hair is acceptable, the cosmetic world has devised this timesaving procedure. The removal of the hair itself is a relatively slow process, but you will never have to wax, shave, or depilitate those areas again!

Electrologists are well paid as this is considered the ultimate treatment in hair removal.

MANICURISTS AND PEDICURISTS

Nail technicians can find employment in beauty salons, hotels, hospitals, barbershops, and even cruise ships. This profession is one of the few beauty services administered while the operator is seated, which is no small consideration if you are putting in eight hours per day. Well manicured nails are a very visible sign of your personal grooming and have often been the deciding factor in making a good impression. How many times have you noticed dirty, unkempt, or bitten nails? Your job as a nail technician can make people feel better about themselves.

SCALP TREATMENT SPECIALISTS

This operator can find employment in a beauty salon, hair treatment salon, or perhaps a barbershop. Another area where the scalp treatment specialist finds work is as a demonstrator for the hair treatment product company. There are many companies that specialize in cosmetic yet therapeutic products to stimulate healthy hair and scalps, and that market their extensive lines in beauty salons, department stores, and specialty boutiques. Some of these products are also sold in pharmacies, particularly in Europe. Scalp treatment has become so scientific that it entails medicated products and thus needs a certified or licensed operator to administer the services.

Schooling for the scalp treatment specialist would be given in a beauty school or could be learned from other specialist instructors in on-the-job training. This is a field where you would probably have to work in a large urban area to attract enough clients to survive financially. The demonstration end of products for scalp treatment would more than likely be a travel job, where you spend most of your time visiting beauty salons throughout the country. This job combined with commissions for all the products that you would be promoting could return a very handsome income.

HAIRDRESSING TEACHER

An instructorship in hairdressing entails a background of cosmetology and the possession of that trade's certification or licensing. Apprenticeship in your chosen field may also be a prerequisite depending upon the province.

A hairdressing teacher can find employment in a beauty school, vocational school, or a technical institute. Instructorship is not like practicing cosmetology; it exacts great patience on the part of the teacher who must convey knowledge of the trade carefully and precisely. There are different benefits to be gained by working in a beauty school versus a vocational or public school. You will want to investigate all the pros and cons of your possible future employment.

Instructorship is a very secure position and can afford a lengthy and enjoyable career. The salary would depend on the area of the country where you choose to live, but again the urban areas probably would offer the most opportunities in this particular field.

FINDING THE RIGHT SCHOOL

There are several associations in Canada that are affiliated with the cosmetological world. It would be quite helpful to contact one or more of these professional groups for information. If they are able to give you some direction, then you can continue your own search for the perfect career for you. Their specialities are varied enough for you to glean details on specific career options and see what avenues interest you. Hairstyling, barbering, and aesthetics are encompassed in these organizations.

For further information you can telephone the Ministry of Education and Training, specifically the Public Inquiry Department, in your particular province.

The provincial Training and Adjustment Board can also be of help. Each province has its own jurisdiction and can guide you.

To make certain that the school you are interested in is a bona fide one, do check with the provincial authorities for certification. It would be a terrible mistake to attend a place for instruction only to discover that it met neither regulatory expectations or yours.

The Canadian Cosmetological Associations follow.

CANADIAN COSMETOLOGICAL ASSOCIATIONS

Alberta Barberstylist Association
    4618 Bownes Rd. NW
    Calgary, AB T3B 0B3

Allied Beauty Association (ABA)
    2 Sheppard Ave. East
    P.O. Box 42, #1001
    North York, ON M2N 5Y7

Association of Nova Scotia Hairdressers (ANSH)
    No. 9, 75 MacDonald Ave.
    Dartmouth, NS B3B 1S5

Barbers Association of British Columbia
    No. 411, 207 Hastings St. West
    Vancouver, BC V6B 1H7

Hairdressers Association of British Columbia
    1777 Third Ave. West
    Vancouver, BC V6J 1K7

New Brunswick Hairdressers Association
    340 Brunswick St.
    Fredricton, NB E3B 1H1

Canadian Society for Aesthetics
    Societe Canadienne d'esthetique (CSA/SCE)
    Atwater Campus, Dawson College
    3432 rue Sherwood Ouest
    Montreal, PQ H3Z 1H4

APPENDIX A

BIBLIOGRAPHY

STATUTES AND LEGAL TEXTS

Wright, John W. and Dwyer, Edward J. *The American Almanac of Jobs and Salaries.* New York: Avon Books, 1990.

The Barbering and Cosmetology Act, State of California (Chapter 10 of Division 3 of the Business and Professions Code), includes Amendments Through January 1, 1995.

Board of Barbering and Cosmetology, New Regulations found in Title 16, Division 9, California Code of Regulations. Authority cited from Business and Professions Code.

Directory of Associations in Canada. Toronto, Ontario, Canada: Micromedia Limited, 1995–1996.

Hopke, William E. *Ninth Edition Encyclopedia of Careers and Vocational Guidance.* Chicago, Illinois: J. G. Ferguson Publishing Company, 1993.

Florida *Department of Business and Professional Regulation* Division of Professions, Board of Cosmetology, *Laws and Rules.* Chapter 477 and Section 455.2228 *Florida Statutes and Rules.* Chapter 61G5, Florida Administrative Code, August 15, 1995.

Hairdressing and Cosmetology, Statutory Provisions, Rules and Regulations, State Sanitary Code, New York City Health Code, Glossary of Terms, Sample Test Questions, Department of State, Division of Licensing Service, Albany, New York.

National Directory of State Business Licensing and Regulations. Detroit Michigan: Gale Research Inc, 1994.

National Occupational Classification, 1992. Minister of Supply and Services. Canada, 1993. Catalogue # MP53-25/1-1993E.

Statistics Canada. Employment Income by Occupation. Ottawa: Industry, Science and Technology Canada, 1993. 1991 Census of Canada Catalogue # 93-332.

State of New York, *An Act,* to amend the general business law in relation to the licensing of the practice of nail specialty, natural hair styling, aesthetics, and cosmetology and to repeal Article 27.

SUGGESTED READING

Books

Brooks, Jessica. *Career After Cosmetology School.* S by S Publications, 1994.

Coletti, Anthony B. *Competency in Cosmetology.* 3rd ed. Keystone Publications, 1990.

Cuaderno Practico Para Texto De Cosmetologia Milady. Milady Publications, 1992.

Eber, Jose. *Beyond Hair: The Ultimate Makeover Book.* Simon & Schuster, 1990.

Edgerton, Leslie. *You and Your Clients: Human Relations for Cosmetology.* Milady Publishers, 1991.

Gerson, Joel. *Standard Textbook for Professional Estheticians.* 7th ed. Milady Publications, 1992.

Hoffman, Lee. *Keep 'em Coming Back: Milady's Guide to Salon Promotion and Client Retention.* Milady Publishers, 1994.

Mataya, Geri. *The Salon Biz: Tips for Success.* Milady Publishing, 1992.

Patton, Jean E. *Color to Color: The Black Woman's Guide to a Rainbow of Fashion and Beauty.* New York, Simon & Schuster, 1991.

Simmons, John V. *The Beauty Salon & Its Equipment.* Macmillan, 1990.

State Board Review Questions: *The Professional Cosmetologist.* 3rd ed. West Publishers, 1991.

Articles

Berg, Rona. "The Softer Touch." *The New York Times Magazine* (Feb 21, 1993, p. S46, col 1).

Cohen, Gad. "Whose Hair Is This, Anyway?" *Mademoiselle* (Feb 1991, p. 124).

Edwards, Owen. "Bad Hair Daze." *Forbes* (Feb 28, 1994).

Gaudoin, Tina. "Makeup's Minirevolution." *Harper's Bazaar* (Jan 1993).

Geibel, Victoria. "Going for Glamour; Making Headlines Today." *Vogue* (July 1991).

Gooden, Charmaine. "Network Hair." *Chatelaine* (Nov 1992).

Gray, Paul. "The Chrome-Dome Scenario." *Time* (Jul 2, 1990).

Gregory, Deborah. "Hair-Raising Tales." *Essence* (Jan 1992).

Hunter, Catherine Ellis. "Have Scissors, Will Travel." *Drug and Cosmetic Industry* (Apr 1993).

Johnson, Lois Joy. "America's 50 Top Hairstylists." *Ladies Home Journal* (Oct 1992).

Logan, Julie. "Americans Are Putting Themselves in the Capable Hands of European Skin-Care Experts." *Vogue* (Apr 1990).

Lord, Shirley. "Anything Goes Was the Message at the Fall Shows." *Vogue* (Jun 1991).

Lord, Shirley. "Real hairdressing is back." *Vogue* (May 1991).

Low, Jennifer. "Hair Tools." *Chatelaine* (Feb 1995).

McCarthy, Flynn. "Pin It On, Tie It Up? There's More Than One Way to Wear the Great New Faux Hairpieces." *Vogue* (Nov 1990).

Min, Janice. "Clip Job." *People Weekly* (Jan 1995).

Myers, Joe. "How to Qualify for the Mane Event." *Ingram's* (Apr 1995).

Nomani, Asra Q. "Knot Here? Dreadlocks Ruled O.K. to Wear to Work." *The Wall Street Journal* (Jul 25, 1995).

Sahag, John. "Shear success!" *McCall's* (Jan 1995).

Shaw, Jessica. "Combing for Trends in Beverly Hills." *Entertainment Weekly* (Oct 21, 1994).

Siroto, Janet. "Lightening Strikes." *Vogue* (Jan 1994).

Stephen, Lynnea Y. "Dangers in African Hair Fashion." *Ms. Magazine* (Jul–Aug 1992).

Sullivan Jr., Robert E. "Male Grooming Has a New Ploy." *Vogue* (Jun 1992).

Trucco, Terry. "Rolling Out of Bed." *The New York Times Magazine* (Nov 24, 1991).

Urquhart, Rachel. "One Woman's Perfect Style Can Be Another's Hair Raising Experience, Leading to Tangled Lawsuits and an Increase in Salon Insurance Costs." *Vogue* (Feb 1992).

APPENDIX B

STANDARDS FOR ACCREDITATION

Accreditation means that a school has met national standards of educational performance which have been established by an impartial nongovernmental agency. Cosmetology schools must meet and maintain the following standards, established by the National Accrediting Commission of Cosmetology Arts and Sciences, in order to be accredited.

The school of cosmetology arts and sciences has well-organized curriculums designed to prepare graduates for licensing examination and for profitable employment.

The ownership and control of the school are publicly stated. Modern methods of organization and administration are employed, and the school is operated on an ethical basis.

Student recruitment reflects sound ethical and legal practices. The school recruits and admits students who have aptitude, interest and motivation to learn and be employable in the field of cosmetology arts and sciences.

Student tuition, fees and refund policies are clearly outlined and completely stated in printed form, and are uniformly administered. Student financial records are maintained, and are current.

The school maintains a supervised and adequately equipped clinic which serves exclusively as a laboratory in which students improve their knowledge and skills in cosmetology science.

The school has a faculty of adequate size qualified by preparation, experience and personality to carry out the objectives of the school.

The school of cosmetology arts and sciences has adequately equipped work stations; secure provisions for storage of equipment, records and supplies; and provides safe working conditions.

The school provides an adequate supply of authoritative and instructional materials and training aids needed in the instruction of each curriculum offered in the overall school program.

Well-developed teaching plans exist for each instructional session, and teaching techniques reflect currently acceptable educational practices.

Each student is given guidance and counseling throughout his or her school career, and assistance in securing employment is provided.

The school is financially sound and able to discharge its responsibilities to its students.

The school is operated as a post-secondary educational institution and maintains the appearance of a school. It must have an officially designated administrative office or center and appropriate classrooms. Areas must be provided for guidance and counseling, library, and other supportive services.

CURRICULA AVAILABLE IN ACCREDITED SCHOOLS

Whether you take your cosmetology education in a private or public school, the curriculum should be quite the same. Your ultimate goal is to acquire your state license and that means that the school of your choosing will have to offer all the courses to qualify for the examination. Make certain that the establishment is bona fide and ask for its credentials before you sign for enrollment or pay any tuition or deposit. If you are uncertain about the school's accreditation and you are fearful or worried about its representation to the public, do inquire about it at the local Better Business Bureau (Look for it in your Yellow Pages.).

A description of some of the curriculum titles used by schools and the general objectives and curriculum descriptions for each code follows.

Advanced Cosmetology

(Schools may use curriculum titles such as: Advanced Cosmetology, Master Cosmetology, Coiffure Creation, Grand Master Hairdresser, Cosmetology II, or Advanced Hairdressing and Cosmetology.)

Objective and curriculum description. The objective of an advanced cosmetology curriculum is to advance the licensed cosmetologist's knowledge and expertise in the industry. Emphasis is placed on improving techniques and perfecting new styles. Instruction is also given on how to improve their financial position in the industry.

Barbering

(Schools may use curriculum titles such as: Barbering, Men's Hairstyling, Barbering/Cosmetology Course, or Barbers Program.)

Objective and curriculum description. The primary objective of the barbering curriculum is to prepare students for the state licensing examination to become a licensed barber. The course of study generally includes cutting and styling, hair coloring, permanent waving, scalp and hair treatments, and shaving. Special emphasis is placed on hair care for men.

Cosmetology

(Schools may use curriculum titles such as: Basic Cosmetology, General Cosmetology, Beauty Culture, Cosmetology, Operator, Hairdressing, Beautician, or Hair Design.)

Objective and curriculum description. The primary objective of the cosmetology curriculum is to prepare students for the state licensing examination to become a licensed cosmetologist. The course of study generally includes cutting and styling, hair coloring, makeup and facials, manicuring and pedicuring, permanent waving, scalp and hair treatments, and other related subjects.

Hair Removal

(Schools may use curriculum titles such as: Hair Removal or Electrolysis.)

Objective and curriculum description. The objective of a hair removal curriculum is to advance the student's knowledge and expertise in the permanent removal of hair. The course of study generally includes machine operation, sanitation and sterilization, posture and positioning, advertisement, salon setups, and ethics.

Hair Weaving

Objective and curriculum description. The objective of the hair weaving curriculum is to advance the student's knowledge and expertise in hair weaving and braiding techniques. Emphasis is place on current styles and creation of new designs.

Manicuring

(Schools may use curriculum titles such as: Manicuring, Cosmetology-Manicurist, Manicurist-Pedicurist, or Manicuring and Sculptured Nails.)

Objective and curriculum description. The objective of the manicuring curriculum is to train the student in nail structures and manicuring techniques. Advanced training may be given in the areas of sculptured nails (application and maintenance), nail wrapping, application of ready-to-wear nails, and pedicuring techniques. Some states have a separate licensing examination for manicurists.

Refresher Training

(Schools may use curriculum titles such as: Refresher Training, Brush-up, or Refresher Beauticians.)

Objective and curriculum description. These curriculums are quite varied and are generally designated to meet the individual needs of individuals for brush-up or refresher training in specific areas of cosmetology to prepare them to take the state examination, obtain a position in the field, or improve specific skills.

Salon Management

(Schools may use curriculum titles such as: Manager, Cosmetology Manager, Junior Manager, Salon Management, Manager Training, Beauty Culture Management, Operator-Manager, Beauty Salon Manager, Master Salon Management, or Beauty Culture Manager.)

Objective and curriculum description. This curriculum is designed to prepare graduate cosmetologists to assume salon management positions or to successfully open their own salons. Emphasis is placed in the areas of good business techniques and practices, common management problems and issues, potential salon problems and their correction and prevention. Some states offer a separate license for salon managers.

Shampoo Specialist

(Schools may use curriculum titles such as: Shampoo Specialist, Shampoo and Conditioning Specialist, Shampoo Technician, or Shampoo Assistant.)

Objective and curriculum description. The purpose of the shampoo specialist curriculum is to train the student in proper shampooing techniques and conditioning of the hair. Emphasis is placed on scalp and skin disorders and product knowledge.

Skin Care

(Schools may use curriculum titles such as: Aesthetician, Cosmetician, Aesthetics, Facialist, Makeup, Master Skin Care and Professional Makeup, or Salon Makeup.)

Objective and curriculum description. The objective of the skin care curriculum is to advance the student's knowledge in the specialized area of skin care and makeup. Special emphasis is placed on diagnosis and treatment of various skin disorders/conditions, professional approach to makeup application, and facial techniques.

Teacher Training

(Schools may use curriculum titles such as: Instructor Training, Junior Instructor, Teacher Trainee, Master Teacher, Student Instructor, Instructor Course, Beauty Culture Teacher, Cadet Teacher, or Theory Instructor.)

Objective and curriculum description. The teacher training curriculum is designed to prepare the licensed cosmetologist to become a licensed instructor. Instruction in public speaking, audiovisual aids, state board of examination, teaching methods, lesson planning, and testing/grading is emphasized.

Unisex

Objective and curriculum description. The purpose of this curriculum is to train the student in the techniques of both men's and women's hair care.

Wig Specialist

(Schools may use curriculum titles such as: Wig Specialist, Wigs, Wiggery, or Wigology.)

Objective and curriculum description. The objective of the wig specialist curriculum is to advance the student's knowledge and expertise in working with wigs and hairpieces. Special emphasis is placed on marketing techniques with the industry, styling, and maintenance of wigs.

Makeup Specialist

(Schools may use curriculum titles such as: Cosmetician, Makeup Specialist.)

Objective and curriculum description. The principle objective in the makeup specialist curriculum is knowing how to apply makeup techniques in the correct and most flattering fashion for each patron. The course usually includes the study of various professional cosmetics, the implements, the principles, and the techniques of makeup application.

Sculptured Nails

(Schools may use curriculum titles such as: Sculptured Nails, Nail Design, Artificial Nails, Advanced Nails.)

Objective and curriculum description. The curriculum generally is designed to train students in advanced nail care, such as nail repair, oil manicures, nail building, and nail wrapping.

Hair Coloring

(Schools may use curriculum titles such as: Hair Coloring, Hair Dying, Permanent Coloring, Hair Tinting, Frosting, Bleaching.)

Objective and curriculum description. The hair coloring curriculum is designed to train the student in the proper techniques used for applying temporary or permanent colors, as well as the steps in lightening or toning a patron's hair.

Hair Cutting

(Schools may use curriculum titles such as: Hair Cutting, Hair Shaping, Advanced Cutting.)

Objective and curriculum description. The primary objective in the hair cutting curriculum is to train students to use the proper implements with the proper technique to give the patron the hairstyle (cut) requested.

Permanent Waving

(Schools may use curriculum titles such as: Body Waving, Cold Waving, Chemical Waving.)

Objective and curriculum description. The permanent waving curriculum is designed to advance the student's knowledge and expertise in the techniques for curling hair. The primary objective is to train students in using professional cold waving chemicals and implements.

African–American Hair Studies

(Schools may use curriculum titles such as: Chemical Relaxing, Hair Straightening, Hair Silking, Hair Pressing.)

Objective and curriculum description. The objective of African–American hair studies is to prepare the student in curl reduction or straightening. Emphasis is usually placed on hair relaxing to permit greater manageability of the hair.

STATE BOARDS OF COSMETOLOGY

Most states (including the District of Columbia and Puerto Rico) have a state cosmetology board which sets requirements for schools, salons, and individual cosmetologists. The rules vary from state to state. For example, the number of hours of training required varies from 1,000 hours (New York, Massachusetts, Colorado, Puerto Rico) to 3,000 hours (New Hampshire). Almost half (23 states) require 1,500 hours. If you want to know the rules for a particular state you should write directly to the state board for this information. The address and telephone number of the state boards is listed below.

ALABAMA BOARD OF COSMETOLOGY
100 Commerce Street, Suite 801
Montgomery, Alabama 36130
(205) 242-5613

ALASKA BOARD OF BARBERS AND HAIRDRESSERS
Department of Commerce and Economic Development
Division of Occupational Licensing
P.O. Box D-LIC
Juneau, Alaska 99811
(907) 465-2541

ARIZONA STATE BOARD OF COSMETOLOGY
1645 W. Jefferson, Room 125
Phoenix, Arizona 85007
(602) 542-5301

ARKANSAS STATE BOARD OF COSMETOLOGY
    1515 West Seventh Street
    Suite 400
    Little Rock, Arkansas 72202
    (501) 682-2168

CALIFORNIA STATE BOARD OF COSMETOLOGY
    Board of Barbering and Cosmetology
    P.O. Box 944226
    Sacramento, California 94244
    (916) 445-7061

COLORADO BOARD OF BARBERS AND COSMETOLOGISTS
    Higher Education Dept.
    Div. of Private Occupational Schools
    1290 Broadway, Ste. 804
    Denver, Colorado 80203
    (303) 894-2960

CONNECTICUT STATE DEPARTMENT OF HEALTH SERVICES
    Division of Medical Quality Assurance
    150 Washington Street
    Hartford, Connecticut 06106
    (203) 566-1042

DELAWARE BOARD OF COSMETOLOGY AND BARBERING
    Dept. of Administrative Services
    Div. of Professional Regulation
    P.O. Box 1401
    Dover, Delaware 19903
    (302) 739-4522

DISTRICT OF COLUMBIA BOARD OF COSMETOLOGY
    Occupational and Professional Licensure Administration
    614 H Street, N.W., Room 1120
    Washington, DC 20001
    (202) 727-7480

FLORIDA STATE BOARD OF COSMETOLOGY
    State Board of Independent Postsecondary Vocational, Technical,
        Trade and Business Schools
    107 Gaines St.
    Tallahassee, Florida 32301
    (904) 488-9504

GEORGIA STATE BOARD OF COSMETOLOGY
Barber and Cosmetology Section
Professional Examining Boards
166 Pryor Street, S.W.
Atlanta, Georgia 30303
(404) 656-3909

HAWAII BOARD OF COSMETOLOGY
Professional and Vocational Licensing Division
Department of Commerce and Consumer Affairs
P.O. Box 3469
Honolulu, Hawaii 96801
(808) 548-3952

IDAHO STATE BOARD OF COSMETOLOGY
Bureau of Occupational Licenses
1109 Main St., Ste. 220
Boise, Idaho 83702
(208) 334-3233

ILLINOIS DEPARTMENT OF PROFESSIONAL REGULATION
320 West Washington Street
3rd Floor
Springfield, Illinois 62786
(217) 782-8556

INDIANA BOARD OF COSMETOLOGY
State Licensing Division
Professional Licensing Agency
1021 State Office Building
100 N. Senate Avenue
Indianapolis, Indiana 46204
(317) 232-2980

IOWA COSMETOLOGY BOARD OF EXAMINERS
Dept. of Public Health
Lucas State Office Building
Des Moines, Iowa 50319
(515) 281-6762

KANSAS STATE BOARD OF COSMETOLOGY
717 Kansas Avenue
Topeka, Kansas 66603
(913) 296-3155

KENTUCKY STATE BOARD OF
HAIRDRESSERS AND COSMETOLOGISTS
 314 W. Second Street
 Frankfort, Kentucky 40601
 (502) 564-4262

LOUISIANA STATE BOARD OF COSMETOLOGY
 11622 Sunbelt Court Industriplex, Room 412
 Baton Rouge, LA 70816
 (504) 568-5267

MAINE STATE BOARD OF COSMETOLOGY
 Dept. of Professional and Financial Regulation
 State House Station 62
 Augusta, Maine 04333
 (207) 582-8745

MARYLAND STATE BOARD OF COSMETOLOGISTS
 Dept. of Licensing and Regulation
 501 St. Paul Place
 Baltimore, Maryland 21202
 (410) 333-6320

MASSACHUSETTS BOARD OF
REGISTRATION OF HAIRDRESSERS
 Div. of Registration
 100 Cambridge Street
 Boston, Massachusetts 02202
 (617) 727-9940

MICHIGAN STATE BOARD OF COSMETOLOGY
 Bureau of Occupational and Professional Regulation
 Dept. of Commerce
 P.O. Box 30018
 Lansing, Michigan 48909
 (517) 373-9153

MINNESOTA DEPARTMENT OF COMMERCE, LICENSING UNIT
 133 E. 7th St.
 St. Paul, Minnesota 55101
 (612) 296-6319

MISSISSIPPI STATE BOARD OF COSMETOLOGY
 P.O. Box 55689
 Jackson, Mississippi 39296
 (601) 354-6623

MISSOURI STATE BOARD OF COSMETOLOGY
   3605 Missouri Blvd.
   P.O. Box 1062
   Jefferson City, Missouri 65102
   (314) 751-2334

MONTANA STATE BOARD OF COSMETOLOGISTS
   111 N. Jackson
   Helena, Montana 59620
   (406) 444-4288

NEBRASKA STATE BOARD OF COSMETOLOGIST EXAMINERS
   301 Centennial Mall South
   P.O. Box 95007
   Lincoln, Nebraska 68509
   (402) 471-2115

NEVADA STATE BOARD OF COSMETOLOGY
   1785 E. Sahara Avenue
   Suite 255
   Las Vegas, Nevada 89104
   (702) 486-6542

NEW HAMPSHIRE BOARD OF COSMETOLOGY
   Health & Welfare Building
   Hazen Drive
   Concord, New Hampshire 03301
   (603) 271-3608

NEW JERSEY BOARD OF COSMETOLOGY AND HAIRSTYLING
   1100 Raymond Boulevard, Rm. 311
   Newark, New Jersey 07102
   (201) 648-2450

NEW MEXICO STATE BOARD OF COSMETOLOGISTS
   Dept. of Regulation and Licensing
   P.O. Box 25101
   725 St. Michael's Dr.
   Santa Fe, New Mexico 87504
   (505) 827-7176

NEW YORK DEPARTMENT OF STATE,
DIVISION OF LICENSING SERVICES
   162 Washington Ave.
   Albany, N.Y. 12231
   (518) 474-2650

NORTH CAROLINA STATE BOARD OF COSMETIC ARTS
4101 North Blvd. Ste. H
Raleigh, North Carolina 27604
(919) 790-8460

NORTH DAKOTA STATE BOARD OF COSMETOLOGY
Box 2177
Bismark, North Dakota 58202
(701) 224-9800

OHIO BOARD OF COSMETOLOGY
8 East Long Street
Suite 1000
Columbus, Ohio 43215
(614) 466-3834

OKLAHOMA STATE BOARD OF COSMETOLOGY
2200 Classen Blvd.
Suite 1530
Oklahoma City, Oklahoma 73106
(405) 521-2441

OREGON STATE BOARD OF BARBERS AND HAIRDRESSERS
750 Front St. NE, Ste. 200
Salem, Oregon 97310
(503) 378-8667

PENNSYLVANIA STATE BOARD OF COSMETOLOGY
Bureau of Professional and Occupational Affairs
Dept. of State
Transportation and Safety Bldg., 6th Fl.
Harrisburg, Pennsylvania 17120
(717) 787-8503

PUERTO RICO BOARD OF EXAMINERS OF
BEAUTY SPECIALISTS
P.O. Box 3271
San Juan, Puerto Rico 00904
(809) 725-0142

RHODE ISLAND STATE BOARD OF HAIRDRESSING
Div. of Professional Regulation
Rhode Island Dept. of Health
3 Capitol Hill
Providence, Rhode Island 02908
(401) 277-2511

SOUTH CAROLINA STATE BOARD OF COSMETOLOGY
  3710 Landmark Drive
  Columbia, South Carolina 29205
  (803) 734-9660

SOUTH DAKOTA COSMETOLOGY COMMISSION
  Dept. of Commerce and Regulation
  P.O. Box 127
  Pierre, South Dakota 57501
  (605) 224-5072

TENNESSEE STATE BOARD OF COSMETOLOGY
  500 James Robertson Pkwy.
  Nashville, Tennessee 37245
  (615) 741-2515

TEXAS COSMETOLOGY COMMISSION
  P.O. Box 26700
  Austin, Texas 78755
  (512) 454-4674

UTAH STATE BOARD OF COSMETOLOGY
  Department of Commerce
  Div. of Occupational and Professional Licensing
  160 E. 300 South
  P.O. Box 45802
  Salt Lake City, Utah 84145
  (801) 530-6628

VERMONT STATE BOARD OF COSMETOLOGY
  Office of Professional Regulation
  109 State Street
  Montpelier, Vermont 05609
  (802) 828-2373

VIRGINIA BOARD OF COSMETOLOGY
  Dept. of Commerce
  3600 W. Broad Street
  Richmond, Virginia 23230
  (804) 367-2175

WASHINGTON STATE DEPT. OF LICENSING
  Professional Licensing Services
  Cosmetology Section
  P.O. Box 9026
  Olympia, Washington 98507
  (206) 586-6387

WEST VIRGINIA STATE BOARD OF
BARBERS AND COSMETOLOGISTS
    1716 Pennsylvania Ave., Ste. 7
    Charleston, West Virginia 25302
    (304) 558-2924

WISCONSIN COSMETOLOGY EXAMINING BOARD
    Regulations and Licensing Dept.
    P.O. Box 8935
    Madison, Wisconsin 53708
    (608) 266-8609

WYOMING STATE BOARD OF COSMETOLOGY
    P.O. Box 4480
    Casper, Wyoming 82604
    (307) 265-2917

COSMETOLOGICAL ASSOCIATIONS AND INFORMATION SOURCES

Aestheticians International Association (AIA)
4447 McKinney Ave.
Dallas, TX 75205

American Beauty Association (ABA)
401 N. Michigan Ave.
Chicago, Il 60611

American Electrology Association
106 Oak Ridge Road
Trumbull, CT 06611

Association of Cosmetologists and Hairdressers (ACH)
811 Monroe
Dearborn, MI 48124

Cosmetology Advancement Foundation (CAF)
208 East 51st Street
New York, NY 10022

Hair International/Associated Master Barbers and
Beauticians of American (HI/AMBBA)
124-B E. Main Street
P.O. Box 273
Palmyra, PA 17078

Intercoiffure American (IA)
540 Robert E. Lee
New Orleans, LA 70124

International Chain Salon Association (ICSA)
P.O. Box 12219
Seattle, WA 98102

International Guild of Professional Electrologists
    202 Boulevard, Suite B
    High Point, NC 27262

Nail Manufacturers Council (NMC)
    c/o American Beauty Association
    401 Michigan Ave.
    Chicago, IL 60611

National Accrediting Commission of Cosmetology Arts and Sciences
    Ste. 900
    901 N. Stuart St.
    Arlington, VA 22203

National Association of Accredited Cosmetology Schools
    5201 Leesburg Pike, Suite 205
    Falls Church, VA 22041

National Barber Career Center
    3839 White Plains Road
    Bronx, NY 10467

National Beauty Career Center
    3 Columbia Circle Drive
    Albany, NY 12212

National Beauty Culturist League (NBCL)
    25 Logan Circle NW
    Washington, DC 20005

National Commission for Electrologist Certification
    96 Westminster Road
    West Hempstead, NY 11552

National Cosmetology Association (NCA)
    3510 Olive Street
    St. Louis, MO 63103

Society of Clinical and Medical Electrologists
    6 Abbott Road
    Wellesley Hills, MA 02181

World International Nail and Beauty Association (WINBA)
    1221 N. Lake View
    Anaheim, CA 92807